THE BOOK OF IRISH LISTS AND TRIVIA

THE BOOK OF IRISH LISTS AND TRIVIA

John Gleeson

Gill and Macmillan

Published in Ireland by
Gill and Macmillan Ltd
Goldenbridge
Dublin 8
with associated companies in
Auckland, Delhi, Gaborone, Hamburg, Harare,
Hong Kong, Johannesburg, Kuala Lumpur, Lagos, London,
Manzini, Melbourne, Mexico City, Nairobi,
New York, Singapore, Tokyo
© John Gleeson 1989
0 7171 1695 6
Designed by Denis Baker
The Unlimited Design Co., Dublin
Print origination by The Type Bureau, Dublin
Printed in Great Britain by The Guernsey Press

Dedicated to my mother
Justine Gleeson (née O'Driscoll)

ACKNOWLEDGMENTS
(Placed in alphabetical order)

Burt Bacharach, Benny Baxter and John Fahy, Maurice Bembridge, Aubrey Bourke, Aimee Gleeson, and all the Gleeson clan, Joe Hunt, Henrik Ibsen (and/or his homonym), T. Ishibashi, Gay McCallion, Mannix MacKenna et al, Henry McNicholas, Paul Maher et al, Rene Moore, Caroline Moydow, Jas Murphy and Emmett O'Rafferty, Etta Place (and her friends Robert and Harry), Mary Quinn, Anita Rosencrantz, Bob and Mary Staed, and Robin Horrell et famille, Irving and Amy Wallace. Last, but only alphabetically, David Wallechinsky. I do not wish to give reasons for these acknowledgments, as those who see that they are included will know why, and those who don't won't mind anyway (I hope).

THE LIE OF THE LAND

If we only had old Ireland over here

10 places the same size as Ireland

(To within 5%, these 10 foreign parts are equal in size to the island of Ireland.)

1. ARUNACHAL PRADESH
   Newly-created (in 1972), this union territory in the North East Assam area of India is 5% smaller than Ireland. Formerly called the North East Frontier Agency, it is in the Himalayas, borders Tibet and Burma, and its population is mainly tribal.

2. AUSTRIA
   The Republic of Austria, in South Central Europe, is almost exactly the same size as Ireland, the difference being only 225 square miles, making it only one-hundredth smaller than Ireland.

3. AZERBAIJAN
   This strife-torn constituent republic of the USSR, is 2½% bigger than Ireland, being 86,661 square kilometres in size, compared to Ireland's 84,431 square kilometres. Its capital is Baku.

4. HOKKAIDO
   Japan's second largest island, lying to the north of the principal island of Honshu, is, at 88,775 square kilometres, only one-twentieth again bigger than Ireland.

5. KOBUK
   A county or census division of Alaska in the United States, Kobuk is 97% the size of Ireland, and yet has a population of less than 5,000 or one person for every six square miles. There are acutally five Alaskan counties bigger than Ireland, and none of these has more than 10,000 inhabitants.

1

6. MAINE
   The Pine Tree State of the United States situated in that country's north-easternmost tip, in New England, is at 33,215 square miles in area, less than 2% bigger than Ireland.

7. SOUTH CAROLINA
   The Palmetto State, ranked at 40th in terms of land area, is less than 5% smaller than Ireland, being 31,055 square miles in area.

8. LAKE SUPERIOR
   The largest sheet of fresh water in the world, and the largest of the Great Lakes of North America; 31,700 square miles in area, or one-fortieth smaller than Ireland. Situated 600 feet above sea-level, it shares both Canadian and United States boundaries.

9. UNITED ARAB EMIRATES
   A federation of Trucial States, formerly independent sheikdoms of Arabia, on the south shore of the Persian Gulf; 32,000 square miles in area, only 1.8% smaller than Ireland. The 7 local divisions, each an autonomous emirate, are Abu Dhabi, Ajman, Dubai, Fujairah, Ras al Khaimah, Sharjah, and Umm al Qaiwain.

10. WEST BENGAL
    The Indian state comprising that part of Bengal allocated to India when it achieved independence in 1947; 4% bigger than Ireland. It is increasingly urban, with Calcutta, its capital, having a population of over 9 million. The state's population is now reaching 60,000,000, making it more than 12 times as populous as Ireland.

High Rise
Ireland's 20 tallest mountains

1. CARRAUNTOOHILL
   Ireland's loftiest mountain is found in the Macgillycuddy's Reeks in Co Kerry. It is 3,414 feet or 1,041 metres in height. Mount Everest, the world's tallest mountain above sea level, is 8½ times the height of Carrauntoohill.

2. BEENKERAGH
   A peak about a mile to the north of Carrauntoohill, this is the second highest in Ireland, being 100 feet lower in height, at 3,314 feet.

3. CAHER
   Just south-west of Carrauntoohill, this peak is 3,200 feet in height.

4. An unnamed peak about 1½ miles east of Carrauntoohill, at 3,141 feet, is Ireland's fourth highest mountain peak.

5. MOUNT BRANDON
   This is the highest peak in Ireland outside the Macgillycuddy's Reeks. Situated about 3 miles south of Brandon Head on the Dingle Peninsula, 3 miles east of the village of Ballydavid, it is 3,127 feet in height.

6. Another unnamed peak in the Macgillycuddy's Reeks, halfway between Carrauntoohill and Purple Mountain, at 3,062 feet is Ireland's sixth tallest mountain.

7. LUGNAQUILLA
   At 3,039 feet in height, this is the tallest mountain in Ireland outside Co Kerry, and therefore Leinster's highest peak. It is situated halfway between Baltinglass and Laragh in Co Wicklow.

8. GALTYMORE or DAWSON'S TABLE
   Outside of Co Kerry, this is Munster's highest peak. On the Tipperary/Limerick border in the Galty Mountains, it is situated about halfway between Tipperary Town and Mitchelstown, each being about 5 miles away. It is 3,018 feet high.

9. BAURTREGAUM
   The highest of the Slieve Mish Mountains, situated at the neck of the Dingle Peninsula, is 2,796 feet high, and is about 3 miles south-east of the village of Camp.

10. SLIEVE DONARD
    Ulster's highest peak, the tallest of the Mourne Mountains, is about 2 miles south of Newcastle, Co Down. Its height has been put at both 2,796 feet, which would make it the same height as the previous peak, and at 2,789 feet.

11. SKREGMORE
    Another peak in the Macgillycuddy's Reeks, and the nearest high peak to Tralee, is 2,790 feet high.

12. MULLAGHCLEEVAUN
    Leinster's second tallest mountain is situated in the middle of the Wicklow Mountains, about 4 miles east of the village of Ballyknockan, which is on the Poulaphouca Reservoir. It is 2,786 feet high.

13. Another unnamed peak, above Curraghmore lake in the Macgillycuddy's Reeks, very near Carrauntoohill, is 2,776 feet in height.

14. BRANDON PEAK
    Just south of Brandon Mountain, at 2,764 feet high, this is the 14th loftiest peak in Ireland.

15. MANGERTON MOUNTAIN
    This is just above the Devil's Punch Bowl, 5 miles south of Killarney, and is 2,756 feet high.

16. PURPLE MOUNTAIN
Separated from the Macgillycuddy's Reeks by the Gap of Dunloe, and above Lough Leane, near Killarney, this is 2,739 feet in height.

17. BEENOSKEE
Situated 4 miles north of Annascaul on the Dingle Peninsula, it is 2,713 feet in height.

17. CAHERCONREE
Situated in the Slieve Mish Mountains, and 9 miles east of Beenoskee, it is the same height as Beenoskee at 2,713 feet.

19. LYRACAPUL
The second highest peak in the Galty Mountains, this is 2,712 feet in height.

20. CORRAGHMORE
This south-westernmost peak of the Macgillycuddy's Reeks, is 2,695 feet in height.

21. MWEELREA
Connacht's highest peak is above the northern entrance of Killary Harbour in Co Mayo, and is 2,688 feet in height, or 819 metres.

County Crests
The highest points in Irish counties, in descending order

COUNTY

1. Kerry — Carrauntoohill, 3,414 feet. This makes Ireland's highest point only half the mean elevation of the American state of Colorado (whose lowest point is only 60 feet lower than Carrauntoohill). Mount Everest is 8½ times the height of this peak.

2. Wicklow — Lugnaquilla, 3,039 feet. Angel Falls, the world's highest waterfalls, in Venezuela, is over 200 feet higher than Lugnaquilla.

3. Limerick — Galtymore, 3,018 feet } *
3. Tipperary — Galtymore, 3,018 feet } *

5. Down — Slieve Donard, 2,796 feet

6. Mayo — Mweelrea, 2,688 feet

7. Carlow — Mount Leinster, 2,610 feet } *
7. Wexford — Mount Leinster, 2,610 feet } *

9. Waterford — Knockmealdown, 2,609 feet

10. Dublin — Kippure, 2,475 feet

11. Donegal — Errigal, 2,466 feet

12. Galway — Benbaun, 2,395 feet

13. Cork — Knockboy, 2,321 feet

14. Derry — Sawel, 2,231 feet

15. Cavan — Cuilcagh, 2,179 feet } *
15. Fermanagh — Cuilcagh, 2,179 feet } *

17.	Sligo	Truskmore, 2,120 feet. (The world's tallest man-made structure, the Warsaw Radio mast, situated 60 miles north-west of Warsaw in Poland, is 8 inches taller than Truskmore.)
18.	Tyrone	Mullaghclogha, 2,080 feet
19.	Leitrim	A point on Truskmore, 2,075 feet
20.	Louth	Slieve Foy, 1,935 feet
21.	Armagh	Slieve Gullion, 1,885 feet
22.	Antrim	Trostan, 1,808 feet
23.	Clare	Glennagallaigh, 1,750 feet
24.	Laois	Arderin, 1,734 feet ⎫ ⋆
24.	Offaly	Arderin, 1,734 feet ⎭ ⋆
26.	Kilkenny	Brandon Hill, 1,703 feet
27.	Monaghan	Mullynash, 1,049 feet. Gavarnie, Europe's highest waterfall, situated in south-west France, is 300 feet taller than Mullynash.
28.	Longford	Corn Hill, 916 feet
29.	Meath	Slieve na Gailligh, 911 feet
30.	Roscommon	Slieve Bawn, 864 feet
31.	Westmeath	Mullaghmeen, 855 feet
32.	Kildare	Dunmurry Hill, 768 feet. (The world's tallest building, the Sears Tower in Chicago, is, without the TV antenna, just slightly short of twice the height of Dunmurry Hill.)

*Peaks on the boundary of two counties

riverrun

Ireland's 22 largest river catchments (in descending order) (measured in square kilometres)

This list includes all rivers with a catchment area in excess of 1,000 square kilometres

	Square Kilometres		Square Kilometres
1. Shannon (This covers a total area ⅞ the size of the province of Connacht, or 18.5% of the island of Ireland.)	15,532	10. Nore	2,530
		11. Moy	2,058
		12. Mourne	1,870
		13. Slaney	1,844
		14. Suck	1,598
2. Bann	5,807	15. Blackwater (Ulster)	1,507
3. Barrow	5,597	16. Liffey	1,370
4. Erne	4,375	17. Inny	1,259
5. Suir	3,572	18. Lee (Cork)	1,254
6. Blackwater (Munster)	3,326	19. Brosna	1,223
7. Corrib	3,139	20. Feale	1,153
8. Foyle	2,924	21. Maigue	1,075
9. Boyne	2,694	22. Clare	1,036

Source: Ordnance Survey

Stepping stones

The 20 largest islands off the Irish coastline, in order of land size

1. ACHILL ISLAND
   Off the coast of Co Mayo, Achill is 56½ square miles in area (or 36,248 acres), making it by far the largest island off the coast of Ireland, and more than 4 times the size of the second biggest island, Inishmore. It also boasts the highest population of the offshore islands, with 3,101 living there in 1981 (in 1961 the population was 5,260).

2. INISHMORE
   The largest of the Aran Islands, off the coast of Co Clare, Inishmore is 9 miles by 2½ miles, roughly 14 square miles in area, or 7,635 acres. The 1981 population was 891 (in the 1961 census the population was 1,768).

3. VALENTIA ISLAND
   (Irish name = Dairbhre, meaning 'Place of Oaks') Valentia, off the Kerry coast, is 6,504 acres in area, measuring 6 or 7 miles long and 2 miles wide, being 10 square miles in area. The 1981 population of the island was 718.

4. GORUMNA ISLAND
   Off the Connemara coast of Co Galway, Gorumna is 5,908 acres in size. Its population in 1981 was 1,122.

5. BERE ISLAND
   (Irish name = an tOilean Mor, meaning 'The Big Island') Bere is in Bantry Bay off the Beara Peninsula. It is 4,381 acres in area, approximately 6.75 square miles. Its population in 1981 was 252.

6. ARAN ISLAND
   (Also called Aranmore Island) Aran lies off the low-lying coast of the Rosses on the Donegal coast, and measures 4 miles by 3, a total of 4,356 acres in area, or 7 square miles. The 1981 population was 803. It is served by motor-boat from Burtonport.

7. CLEAR ISLAND
Off the Cork coast, Clear is 4,033 acres in area. The population of the island in 1981 was 164. Fasnet Rock, with its lighthouse, lies 4 miles south-west of Cape Clear, a familiar landmark for seamen.

8. CLARE ISLAND
At the entrance to Clew Bay in Co Mayo, Clare is 4,024 acres in area, about 6.25 square miles. The population of the island was 127 in 1981.

9. RATHLIN ISLAND
Off the northern coast of Co Antrim, Rathlin measures 3,564 acres, or about 5½ square miles.

10. LETTERMORE ISLAND
Off the coast of Co Galway, Lettermore is 2,253 acres in area. The 1981 population was 585.

11. INISHMAAN
(Meaning 'middle island'). This is the second largest of the Aran Islands and is 2,252 acres in area. The 1981 population was 238, from 361 in 1961.

12. INISHBOFIN
(Meaning 'The Island of the White Cow') Inishbofin lies off the coast of Connemara, is 2,374 acres in area or about 3.75 square miles. The 1981 population of the island was 195.

13. DURSEY ISLAND
Dursey lies off the end of the Beara Peninsula in Co Cork and is 1,402 acres in area, just over 2 square miles. Its population in 1981 was only 19.

14. SHERKIN ISLAND
(Meaning 'Arcan's Island'), Sherkin lies between Baltimore, Co Cork, and Clear Island. It is 1,247 acres in area. The population of the island in 1981 was 70.

15. INISHEER
(Meaning 'Island of the East'). This is the smallest of the Aran Islands, measuring 1,148 acres in area. (The Aran Islands' total area is 18 square miles.) Its population in 1981 was 239, one more than Inishmaan. In 1961 there were 376 inhabitants on the island.

16. GREAT BLASKET
This is the largest of Kerry's Blasket Islands. It is 1,132 acres in area, being 4 miles long but very narrow, and rising to 960 feet.

17. WHIDDY ISLAND
Whiddy lies in Bantry Bay and is approximately 1,000 acres in area. In 1981 it had a population of 54.

18. RINGAROGY ISLAND
Ringarogy in Roaringwater Bay, Co Cork, is 950 acres in area, and in 1981 had 69 inhabitants.

19. INISHTURK
North-east from the island of Inishbofin (see above), off the coast of Co Galway, Inishturk is 650 acres in area. In 1981 the population was only 7.

20. TORY ISLAND
(Meaning 'Place of Towers'). Lying off the northern coast of Donegal Tory is 3 miles long, less than a mile wide, and is 7 miles from the nearest point on the mainland. The 1961 population was 273, and had fallen to 208 by 1981.

From Bantry Bay up to Derry Quay And from Galway to Dublin town

Ireland's 32 counties in order of size

Below are the 32 counties of Ireland placed in order of size, and where possible, they are compared in size to other places around the world.

1. CORK

At 3,820 square miles (or 1,843,300 acres), it is 9 times the size of the smallest county, Louth. It is larger than the total area of the Canary or Hebrides Islands, is 90% the size of the island of Crete, and slightly larger than the island of Mindanao in the Philippines.

2. GALWAY

The largest county in Connacht, it measures 1,467,000 acres and is larger than the English county of Lincolnshire.

3. MAYO

Connacht's second largest county, it is bigger than the total area of the Balearic Islands, the same size as Bali, and is bigger than the state of Delaware in the United States.

4. DONEGAL

The largest county in Ulster, at 1,876 square miles, it is bigger than the island of Trinidad, and is the same size as the Canadian province of Prince Edward Island.

5. KERRY

At 1,161,700 acres in size, it is Munster's second largest county.

6. TIPPERARY

The smallest of the 6 counties which contain over a million acres, it is Munster's third largest. It is bigger than the island of Long Island, in New York state.

7. TYRONE   Northern Ireland's biggest county, and Ulster's second largest, its area is 806,919 acres, and it is slightly smaller than the island of South Georgia in the South Atlantic.

8. CLARE   At 787,700 acres it is Munster's fourth biggest county. It is larger than the smallest state in the United States, Rhode Island.

9. ANTRIM   The second largest county in Northern Ireland, it is the third largest in Ulster. Equal in size to the county of Lancashire, it is slightly smaller than the islands of Samoa.

10. LIMERICK   At 1,064 square miles it is closest in size to the average size of an Irish county. The second smallest county in Munster, it is larger than the country of Luxembourg.

11. DOWN   At 952 square miles, it is Ulster's fourth largest, and Northern Ireland's third biggest county. It is slightly smaller than Réunion Island in the Indian Ocean.

12. ROSCOMMON   Less than 1,000 acres smaller than Co Down, at 609,000 acres, it is slightly bigger than Co Durham in England. It is Connacht's third largest county.

13. WEXFORD   Leinster's biggest county, at 581,000 acres, it is less than one-third the size of Co Cork. It is larger than all the islands of the Azores put together.

14. MEATH   At 905 square miles in area, it is Leinster's second largest county, and is bigger than Cheshire, in England.

15. DERRY   At 523,000 acres in area, it is Ulster's fifth largest county, being slightly smaller than Nottinghamshire.

16. KILKENNY	Just over half a million acres in size, and the third largest county in Leinster, it is the same size as the island of Tenerife, and is bigger than the island of Mauritius.
17. WICKLOW	At 500,300 acres, and bigger than West Yorkshire, it is Leinster's fourth biggest county.
18. OFFALY	At 771 square miles or 493,600 acres, it is the fifth largest county in the province of Leinster.
19. CAVAN	Ulster's sixth largest county, Cavan is larger than the English county of Buckinghamshire.
20. FERMANAGH	Northern Ireland's second smallest county, and Ulster's seventh largest, it is slightly smaller than the Indian Ocean archipelago, the Comoro Islands.
21. WATERFORD	Munster's smallest county is 454,100 acres in area, about 713 square miles.
22. SLIGO	Connacht's fourth largest, or second smallest county, Sligo is almost exactly the same size, at 709 square miles, as the English county of East Sussex.
23. WESTMEATH	Leinster's sixth largest county, it is larger than the isle of Skye, and larger than Stewart Island, New Zealand's third largest island.
24. LAOIS	Slightly larger than Sydney, Australia which in area is the world's largest city, Laois is the seventh largest county in Leinster.
25. KILDARE	Bigger than Zanzibar Island, and also Surrey, Kildare is Leinster's eighth largest county.

26. LEITRIM — Connacht's smallest county, at 613 square miles, Leitrim is larger in area than the Faroe Islands, and also bigger than the Hawaiian island of Oahu, which contains Honolulu.

27. ARMAGH — Northern Ireland's smallest and Ulster's second smallest county, Armagh is bigger than the metropolitan county of Greater Manchester, and is slightly smaller than the island of Rhodes.

28. MONAGHAN — Ulster's smallest county, at 318,990 acres, is bigger than Berkshire, England, and slightly smaller than the Scottish region of Fife.

29. LONGFORD — At 403 square miles, Co Longford is the ninth biggest county in Leinster. It is bigger than the Orkney Islands, the same size as Tahiti, and almost exactly the area of Hong Kong.

30. DUBLIN — Although the country's most populated county, it is the third smallest, and is the size of Tyne and Wear and the Isle of Wight put together.

31. CARLOW — At 221,500 acres, Carlow is Leinster's and Ireland's second smallest county.

32. LOUTH — At 202,800 acres, or just under 317 square miles, Louth is Leinster's and Ireland's smallest county. It is, however, bigger than the total area of the Madeira Islands, bigger than Guam, and bigger than the Isle of Man, which is only 140,000 acres.

Living off the land

Irish counties in order of population density
(in persons per square mile)

1. Dublin
   2,875 (Or 4.5 persons to every acre). This is 3 times the density of the most densely populated state in the United States, New Jersey. The Portuguese territory of Macao on the southern coast of China, is 20 times more densely populated than Dublin, with over 90 persons living on every acre of land.

2. Antrim
   590

3. Down
   415

4. Louth
   289

5. Derry
   253

6. Armagh
   239

7. Kildare
   177

8. Tyrone
   158

9. Limerick
   154 (More densely populated than California at 151, and equal in population density to the most sparsely populated English county, Northumberland.)

10. Waterford
    127

11. Wicklow
    121

12. Carlow
    118

13. Meath
    114

14. Wexford
    112

15. Cork
    108

16. Monaghan
    104

17. Kilkenny
    91.8

18. Westmeath
    91.5

19. Tipperary
    83.1

20. Laois
    80

21. Sligo
    79

22. Longford
    78

23. Offaly
    77.6

24. Galway
    75

25. Cavan
    74

26. Clare
    72

27. Fermanagh
    71

28. Donegal
69

29. Kerry
67

30. Roscommon
55

31. Mayo
53

32. Leitrim
44 (Or one person for every 7.5 acres of land, or one sixty-fifth the density of Dublin). Leitrim is more densely populated than the states of Arkansas, Maine, Oregon, and is the same as Oklahoma in the United States.

Source, Census: Republic of Ireland 1986
Northern Ireland 1980

Beasts and fowl
Livestock numbers in the Republic, December 1987

	1988 (Dec)	1977 (Dec)
Cattle	5,579,700	6,245,500
Sheep	3,251,600	2,526,000
Pigs	960,200	997,500
Turkeys	998,200	652,900
Geese	54,000	80,700
Ducks	138,000	198,800
Ordinary Fowl	7,445,800	8,349,000

Source: The annual livestock enumeration, by the Central Statistics Office

Ireland's Most Common Birds

These 13 birds are, according to the following criteria, the most likely to be seen in Ireland:

a. Abundant   b. Resident   c. Widespread   d. All year round

1. Blackbird
2. Chaffinch
3. Dunnock
   (Hedge Sparrow)
4. Goldcrest
5. House Sparrow
6. Jackdaw
7. Magpie
8. Meadow Pipit
9. Reed Bunting
10. Robin
11. Skylark
12. Starling
13. Wood Pigeon

CITY LIMITS

Figures in parentheses place the town in order of population for its county. In the case of Dublin (since comparing towns like Swords to suburbs like Castleknock is not practical), and Northern Ireland (since the data is over 9 years old), no indication is given about comparative sizes of towns in these areas.

Distribution of souls

List 1. Ireland's 41 towns over 10,000 population

1. 502,749
   Dublin City (Dublin County Borough) (Dublin County = 518,700)

2. 416,679
   Belfast

3. 173,694
   Cork

4. 75,276
   Limerick

5. 62,697
   Derry

6. 56,149
   Newtownabbey, Co Antrim

7. 54,715
   Dun Laoghaire, Co Dublin

8. 52,519
   Craigavon (with Lurgan + Portadown), Armagh Larne = 18,224, Portadown = 21,333

9. 46,585
   Bangor, Co Down

10. 41,861
    Galway, Co Dublin

11. 40,391
    Lisburn, Co Antrim

12. 39,529
    Waterford, Co Waterford (1st)

13. 30,508
    Dundalk, Co Louth (1st)

14. 28,166
    Ballymena, Co Antrim

15. 26,103
    Bray, Co Wicklow (1st)

16. 24,681
    Drogheda, Co Louth (2nd)

17. 22,342
    Antrim, Co Antrim

18. 20,531
    Newtownards, Co Down

19. 19,026
    Newry, Co Down

20. 18,018
    Sligo, Co Sligo (1st)

21. 17,633
    Carrickfergus, Co Antrim

22. 17,620
    Tralee, Co Kerry (1st)

23. 17,537
    Kilkenny, Co Kilkenny (1st)

24. 15,967
    Coleraine, Co Derry

25. 15,571
    Athlone, Co Westmeath (1st)

26. 15,547
    Ennis, Co Clare (1st)

27. 15,365
    Wexford, Co Wexford (1st)

28. 15,312
    Swords, Co Dublin

29. 14,895
    Clonmel, Co Tipperary (1st)

30. 14,655
    Dunmurry, Co Antrim

31. 14,627
    Omagh, Co Tyrone

32. 13,816
    Carlow, Co Carlow (1st)

33. 12,700
    Armagh, Co Armagh

34. 12,259
    Lucan, Co Dublin

35. 12,127
    Mullingar, Co Westmeath
    (2nd)

36. 11,938
    Leixlip, Co Kildare (1st)

37. 11,929
    Navan, Co Meath (1st)

38. 11,503
    Newbridge, Co Kildare (2nd)

39. 10,429
    Enniskillen, Co Fermanagh

40. 10,017
    Naas, Co Kildare (3rd)

41. 10,189
    Killarney, Co Kerry (2nd)

List 2. 45 towns with population between 5,000 and 9,999

9,940	Malahide, Co Dublin	7,600	Comber, Co Down
9,809	Letterkenny, Co Donegal (1st)	7,537	Balbriggan, Co Dublin
9,650	Banbridge, Co Down	7,338	Thurles, Co Tipperary (2nd)
9,505	Greystones, Co Wicklow (2nd)	7,135	Celbridge, Co Kildare (4th)
9,462	Holywood, Co Down	6,949	Dungarvan, Co Waterford (2nd)
9,442	Tullamore, Co Offaly (1st)	6,864	Skerries, Co Dublin
9,325	Strabane, Co Tyrone	6,548	Longford, Co Longford (1st)
9,055	Portmarnock, Co Dublin		
8,490	Ballina, Co Mayo (1st)	6,357	New Ross, Co Wexford (3rd)
8,388	Arklow, Co Wicklow (3rd)	6,284	Monaghan, Co Monaghan (1st)
8,384	Portlaoise, Co Laois (1st)	6,246	Newcastle, Co Down
8,295	Dungannon, Co Tyrone	6,140	Ballinasloe, Co Galway (2nd)
8,282	Cobh, Co Cork (2nd)	6,114	Midleton, Co Cork (4th)
8,254	Downpatrick, Co Down	6,039	Tuam, Co Galway (3rd)
8,015	Limavady, Co Derry	6,036	Kilkeel, Co Down
8,005	Shannon, Co Clare (2nd)	5,999	Tramore, Co Waterford (3rd)
7,753	Enniscorthy, Co Wexford (2nd)	5,952	Youghal, Co Cork (5th)
7,685	Mallow, Co Cork (3rd)	5,893	Carrigaline, Co Cork (6th)
7,655	Castlebar, Co Mayo (2nd)	5,777	Nenagh, Co Tipperary (3rd)

5,679	Ballymoney, Co Antrim	5,312	Portstewart, Co Derry
5,498	Wicklow, Co Wicklow (4th)	5,219	Cavan, Co Cavan (1st)
5,449	Athy, Co Kildare (5th)	5,209	Tipperary, Co Tipperary (5th)
5,352	Carrick-on-Suir, Co Tipperary (4th)	5,114	Portrush, Co Antrim

List 3. Populations between 2,501 and 5,000

4,926	Bandon, Co Cork (7th)	3,674	Newcastle West, Co Limerick (2nd)
4,885	Maynooth, Co Kildare (6th)	3,591	Randalstown, Co Antrim
4,885	Fermoy, Co Cork (8th)	3,558	Ardee, Co Louth (3rd)
4,513	Rush, Co Dublin	3,473	Roscommon, Co Roscommon (1st)
4,378	Roscrea, Co Tipperary (6th)	3,465	Ashbourne, Co Meath (3rd)
4,268	Kildare, Co Kildare (8th)	3,465	Carrickmacross, Co Monaghan (2nd)
4,194	Birr, Co Offaly (2nd)		
4,131	Buncrana, Co Donegal (2nd)	3,456	Westport, Co Mayo (3rd)
4,124	Trim, Co Meath (2nd)	3,360	Loughrea, Co Galway (4th)
3,884	Gorey, Co Wexford (4th)	3,294	Portarlington, Co Laois (2nd)
3,874	Donaghadee, Co Down		
3,753	Edenderry, Co Offaly (3rd)	3,321	Laytown-Bettystown-Mornington, Co Louth (5th)
3,721	Ballynahinch, Co Down		
3,704	Passage West, Co Cork (9th)	3,210	Mitchelstown, Co Cork (10th)
3,693	Ceannanas Mor (Kells), Co Meath (3rd)	3,130	Mountmellick, Co Laois (2nd)
3,693	Listowel, Co Kerry (3rd)	3,089	Dromore, Co Down

3,035	Castleblayney, Co Monaghan (3rd)	2,811	Bantry, Co Cork (12th)
3,015	Ballyshannon, Co Donegal (3rd)	2,788	Muine Bheag, Co Carlow (2nd)
2,991	Rathcoole, Co Dublin	2,786	Clonakilty, Co Cork (13th)
2,961	Kilrush, Co Clare (3rd)	2,756	Bessbrook, Co Armagh
2,928	Ballybofey-Stranorlar, Co Donegal (4th)	2,736	Clara, Co Offaly (5th)
		2,666	Carryduff, Co Down
2,828	Cashel, Co Tipperary (7th)	2,581	Kinsale, Co Cork (14th)
2,814	Charleville (Rath Luirc), Co Cork (11th)	2,561	Keady, Co Armagh
		2,517	Mossley, Co Antrim

Capital shifts

Population of Dublin areas (electoral) in order of size

Dublin City

Population

53,637	Donaghmeade	39,017	Crumlin
49,222	Drumcondra	38,322	Ballyfermot
47,506	Clontarf	37,295	Rathmines
44,172	North Inner City	31,433	Cabra
42,403	Artane	502,749	Total population of Dublin City (Dublin County Borough) (decrease of − 7.7% population since 1981)
40,480	Pembroke		
40,045	South Inner City		
39,217	Finglas		

Dublin County

Population

34,152	Ballybrack	24,934	Dundrum
33,177	Dun Laoghaire	23,822	Blackrock
31,516	Lucan	23,163	Swords
31,470	Terenure	22,628	Mulhuddart
29,734	Clondalkin	22,537	Glencullen
28,322	Tallaght-Oldbawn	22,191	Howth
27,493	Balbriggan	21,703	Malahide
27,344	Greenhills	21,301	Castleknock
25,779	Tallaght-Rathcoole	16,838	Clonskeagh
25,381	Rathfarnham	518,700	Total population outside Dublin city (+ 13.2% increase since 1981)
25,215	Stillorgan		

Ebb and Flow

Towns with biggest increases and losses in population 1981–1986

These are the towns in the Republic of Ireland, with a population of more than 3,000, which have increased or decreased most in population in the 5 year period between 1981 and 1986.

% increase		% decrease	
+ 54.9	Celbridge, Co Dublin	– 4.0	Thurles, Co Tipperary
+ 44.0	Ashbourne, Co Meath	– 3.9	Ballina, Co Mayo
+ 40.7	Maynooth, Co Kildare	– 3.8	Carrick-on-Suir, Co Tipperary
+ 40.5	Carrigaline, Co Cork	– 3.6	Mountmellick, Co Laois
+ 36.0	Swords, Co Dublin		
+ 28.5	Leixlip, Co Dublin	– 3.4	Nenagh, Co Tipperary
+ 20.0	Naas, Co Kildare	– 3.0	Birr, Co Offaly
+ 19.9	Greystones, Co Wicklow	– 3.0	Arklow, Co Wicklow
+ 16.7	Skerries, Co Dublin	– 3.0	Portarlington, Co Laois
+ 16.5	Rush, Co Dublin	– 3.0	Youghal, Co Cork
+ 14.6	Trim, Co Meath		
+ 12.2	Letterkenny, Co Donegal		
+ 11.2	Bray, Co Wicklow		
+ 10.8	Laytown-Bettystown-Mornington, Co Louth		
+ 10.4	Portmarnock, Co Dublin		

Pride of Place

Ireland's Tidy Towns winners since the scheme was inaugurated in 1958

1.	1958	Glenties, Co Donegal
2.	1959	Glenties, Co Donegal
3.	1960	Glenties, Co Donegal
4.	1961	Rathvilly, Co Carlow
5.	1962	Glenties, Co Donegal
6.	1963	Rathvilly, Co Carlow
7.	1964	Virginia, Co Cavan
8.	1965	Virginia, Co Cavan
9.	1966	Ballyjamesduff, Co Cavan
10.	1967	Ballyjamesduff, Co Cavan
11.	1968	Rathvilly, Co Carlow
12.	1969	Tyrrellspass, Co Westmeath
13.	1970	Malin, Co Donegal
14.	1971	Ballyconnell, Co Cavan
15.	1972	Trim, Co Meath
16.	1973	Kiltegan, Co Wicklow
17.	1974	Trim, Co Meath
18.	1975	(a tie) Ballyconnell, Co Cavan
		Kilsheelan, Co Tipperary
19.	1976	Adare, Co Limerick
20.	1977	Multyfarnham, Co Westmeath

23.	1980	Newtowncashel, Co Longford
24.	1981	Mountshannon, Co Clare
25.	1982	Dunmanway, Co Cork
26.	1983	Terryglass, Co Tipperary
27.	1984	Trim, Co Meath
28.	1985	Kilkenny City, Co Kilkenny
29.	1986	Kinsale, Co Cork
30.	1987	Sneem, Co Kerry
31.	1988	Carlingford, Co Louth
32.	1989	Ardagh, Co Longford

Of the 22 different towns to have won up to 1989, 9 are in Leinster, 7 are in Munster, 6 in Ulster, and none in Connacht. Cavan is the only county to have 3 different winners.

The town to have most wins is Glenties (with 4 wins in the first 5 years of the scheme), followed by 3 wins by both Rathvilly (1961, 1963, 1968) and Trim (1972, 1974, 1984) making it the only town to win in 2 decades. Towns with 2 wins include Virginia, Ballyjamesduff, Ballyconnell (one in a tie), and Kilsheelan (one in a tie).

WHAT'S IN A NAME?

Naming of Parts
Nicknames of Irish placenames

1.	Armagh	The Orchard of Ireland
2.	Athlone	The Heart of Ireland
3.	Ballymena	The Aberdeen of Ireland
4.	Bangor	Belfast by the Sea
5.	Belfast	The Athens of Ireland
6.	Ben Bulben	Ireland's Table Mountain
7.	Blasket Islands	The Next Parish to America
8.	Borris-in-Ossory	The Gate of Munster
9.	Bray	The Gateway to the Garden of Ireland
10.	Carlow	The Garden of Erin
11.	Clare	The Banner County
12.	Clifden	Capital of Connemara
13.	Cork	The Drisheen City
14.	Derry	The Maiden City
15.	Dingle	The Most Westerly Town in Europe
16.	Donegal	O'Donnell's Country
17.	Galway	The City of Tribes
18.	Glassan	The Village of the Roses
19.	Killarney	Heaven's Reflex
20.	Kerry	The Kingdom

21.	Limerick	The City of the Violated Treaty
22.	Lissoy	Sweet Auburn
23.	Magilligan	The Medicine Garden of Ireland
24.	Mallow	The Irish Bath
25.	Meath	The Royal County
26.	Monaghan	Farney County

31 old names for Irish towns etc.

	Present name	Old name
1.	Ballydesmond, Co Cork	Kingwilliamstown
2.	Birr, Co Offaly	Parsonstown
3.	Bunclody, Co Wexford	Newtownbarry
4.	Caledon, Co Tyrone	Kennard
5.	Castlebellingham, Co Louth	Garlandstown
6.	Cobh, Co Cork	Queenstown
7.	Daingean, Co Offaly	Philipstown
8.	Draperstown, Co Derry	The Cross
9.	Dublin	Eblana
10.	Dun Laoghaire, Co Dublin	Kingstown
11.	Edenderry, Co Offaly	Coolestown
12.	Edgeworthstown, Co Longford	Mostrim
13.	Eglington, Co Derry	Muff
14.	Fivemiletown, Co Tyrone	Mountstewart

15.	Galway	Magnata
16.	Kenmare, Co Kerry	Neidin
17.	County Laois	Royal County
18.	Lisburn, Co Antrim	Lisnagarvey
19.	County Meath	King's County
20.	Muine Bheag, Co Carlow	Bagenalstown
21.	Newmarket, Co Cork	Ahahasne
22.	Newmills, Co Tyrone	Tullaniskin
23.	Portarlington, Co Laois	Coltodry
24.	Portlaoise, Co Laois	Maryborough, also Fort Protector
25.	Raithluirc, Co Cork	Charleville
26.	Randalstown, Co Antrim	Mainwater, and Ironworks
27.	Riverstown, Co Cork	Ballynarosheen, also Sadlierstown
28.	Rutland Island, Co Donegal	Inishmacdurn
29.	Terenure, Co Dublin	Roundtown
30.	Wicklow	Wykinglo
31.	Wexford	Menapia

Naming of People
The 6 most common surnames in each of the 32 counties

1. ANTRIM (= Solitary Farm)
   1. Smith 2. Johnston 3. Stewart 4. Wilson 5. Thompson 6. O'Neill

2. ARMAGH (= Height of Macha)
   1. Murphy 2. Hughes 3. Wilson 4. Campbell 5. O'Hare 6. Smith

3. CARLOW (= Quadruple Lake)
   1. Murphy 2. Byrne 3. Doyle 4. Nolan 5. Neill 6. Brennan

4. CAVAN (= Hollow)
   1. O'Reilly 2. Smith 3. Brady 4. Lynch 5. McCabe 6. Clarke

5. CLARE (= Plain)
   1. McMahon 2. McNamara 3. Moloney 4. O'Brien
   5. McInerney 6. Kelly

6. CORK (= Marshy Place)
   1. O'Sullivan 2. Murphy 3. McCarthy 4. O'Mahony
   5. O'Donovan 6. Kelly

7. DERRY (= Oak Wood)
   1. O'Doherty 2. McLoughlin 3. Kelly 4. Bradley
   5. Brown 6. McCloskey

8. DONEGAL (= Fortress of the Foreigners)
   1. Gallagher 2. O'Doherty 3. Boyle 4. O'Donnell
   5. McLoughlin 6. Sweeney

9. DOWN (= Fort)
   1. Thompson 2. Smith 3. Campbell 4. Patterson
   5. Martin 6. Wilson

10. DUBLIN (= Black Pool)
    1. Byrne 2. Kelly 3. Doyle 4. Murphy 5. O'Brien 6. Kavanagh

11. FERMANAGH (= Men of Monach)
    1. Maguire 2. McManus 3. Dolan 4. McGovern
    5. McHugh 6. Johnston

12. GALWAY (= Stoney River)
    1. Kelly 2. Burke 3. Conneely 4. Joyce 5. McDonagh 6. Walsh

13. KERRY (= Ciar's People)
    1. O'Sullivan 2. O'Connor 3. O'Shea 4. Murphy
    5. McCarthy 6. Moriarty

14. KILDARE (= Church of the Oak)
    1. Kelly 2. Murphy 3. Dunne 4. Byrne 5. Nolan 6. O'Connor

15. KILKENNY (= St Kenneth)
    1. Brennan 2. Walsh 3. Murphy 4. Ryan 5. O'Carroll 6. Byrne

16. LEITRIM (= Grey Ridge)
    1. Kelly 2. Reynolds 3. Flynn 4. McLoughlin
    5. McHugh 6. Rooney

17. LAOIS (= Laeight's Tribe)
    1. Dunne 2. Delany 3. Conroy 4. Lalor 5. Phelan 6. Fitzpatrick

18. LIMERICK (= Bare Spot)
    1. O'Brien 2. Fitzgerald 3. Sullivan 4. Hayes 5. Walsh 6. Collins

19. LONGFORD (= Fortified Place)
    1. Reilly 2. Farrell 3. Kiernan 4. Kelly 5. O'Donoghue 6. Murphy

20. LOUTH (= River Lud)
    1. Byrne 2. Kelly 3. Murphy 4. Smith 5. Clarke 6. Duffy

21. MAYO (= Plain of the Yew)
    1. Walsh 2. Gallagher 3. Kelly 4. O'Malley 5. Moran 6. Duffy

22. MEATH (= The Middle)
    1. O'Reilly 2. Smith 3. Lynch 4. Brady 5. Farrell 6. Farrelly

23. MONAGHAN (= Little Shrubbery)
    1. Duffy 2. Connolly 3. McMahon 4. McKenna
    5. Hughes 6. Murphy

24. OFFALY (= People of Failghe)
    1. Molloy 2. O'Carroll 3. Kelly 4. Dunne 5. Daly 6. Egan

25. ROSCOMMON (= Wood of Conan)
   1. Kelly 2. McDermott 3. O'Brien 4. Kennedy 5. Dwyer 6. Hogan

26. SLIGO (= Shelly River)
   1. Brennan 2. McLoughlin 3. Gallagher 4. Kelly
   5. Harte 6. McGowan

27. TIPPERARY (= Wood of Ara)
   1. Ryan 2. Maher 3. O'Brien 4. Kennedy 5. Dwyer 6. Hogan

28. TYRONE (= Owen's County)
   1. Quinn 2. Mullan 3. Kelly 4. Donnelly 5. Gallagher 6. McKenna

29. WATERFORD (= Inlet of Wether)
   1. Power 2. Walsh 3. O'Brien 4. Murphy 5. Ryan 6. McGrath

30. WESTMEATH (= Middle West)
   1. Lynch 2. Farrell 3. O'Reilly 4. Daly 5. Murray 6. Duffy

31. WEXFORD (= Inlet by the Sea-washed Bank)
   1. Murphy 2. Doyle 3. Walsh 4. Byrne 5. Cullen 6. Kavanagh

32. WICKLOW (= Meadow of the Vikings)
   1. Byrne 2. Doyle 3. Murphy 4. Kelly 5. Kavanagh 6. Nolan

NB All surnames with varieties, like Reilly and O'Reilly, are grouped together.
Source: *Irish Family Names* (Brian de Breffny)

Toffs
Ireland's most common Christian names, 1988

Below are listed the results of a survey, by Hector Legge, in which he added up the names given by parents to new babies born in 1988, as placed in the notices columns in Saturday's editions of the *Irish Times* of that year.

	Boys			Girls	
1.	David	37 entries	1.	Sarah	24 entries
2.	Conor	20	2.	Rachel	21
2.	Mark	20	3.	Laura	18
4.	John	18	4.	Emma	17
4.	Robert	18	4.	Jennifer	17
6.	Andrew	17	6.	Ashling	16
7.	Stephen	16	7.	Rebecca	15
8.	Christopher	15	8.	Kate	13
9.	Michael	14	9.	Jessica	12
9.	Patrick	14	10.	Clara	8
11.	Simon	13	10.	Claire	8
12.	Kevin	11	10.	Danielle	8
12.	Philip	11	10.	Karen	8
12.	Sean	11	10.	Ruth	8

hoi polloi

The 25 most common surnames in the Republic of Ireland

Below, according to their numbers in the telephone directory, are the 25 most common surnames in the Republic of Ireland. Placed in order, the figure given after each entry is the accumulated number of entries in the directory (Part 1 from 1989 and Part 2 from 1985, the last time a full Part 2 was issued) for each surname.

1.	Murphy	6,992	(1st in Carlow and Wexford)
2.	O'Connor	5,275	
3.	Kelly	4,677	(1st in Galway, Kildare, Leitrim, Roscommon)
4.	O'Brien	4,302	(1st in Limerick)
5.	Ryan	4,210	(1st in Tipperary)
6.	Walsh	3,997	(1st in Mayo)
7.	Byrne	3,939	(1st in Dublin, Louth, Wicklow)
8.	O'Sullivan	3,515	(1st in Cork and Kerry)
9.	McCarthy	2,962	
10.	O'Neill	2,623	
11.	Doyle	2,617	
12.	Lynch	2,197	(1st in Westmeath)
13.	O'Reilly	2,075	(1st in Cavan, Longford, Meath)
14.	Fitzgerald	2,000	

15.	O'Connell	1,910	
16.	Kennedy	1,814	
17.	Brennan	1,803	(1st in Kilkenny and Sligo)
18.	Murray	1,789	
19.	Dunne	1,787	(1st in Laois)
20.	Daly	1,711	
21.	Nolan	1,647	
22.	Collins	1,583	
23.	Kavanagh	1,490	
24.	O'Leary	1,414	
25.	Farrell	1,400	

The figures in brackets are, according to *Irish Family Names* by Brian de Breffny, the most common surnames in each of the counties mentioned. It should be noted that surnames that also have a variety (e.g. Kelly and O'Kelly or Reilly and O'Reilly), are bunched together in this source. The most common surnames in the missing counties, according to this source, are:

Clare : McMahon

Donegal : Gallagher

Monaghan : Duffy

Offaly : Molloy

Waterford : Power

25 most common surnames in Dublin Telephone Directory (1988/89) (measured in number of columns, 6 per leaf, filled)

		Columns	Names
1.	Byrne	26	2,366
2.	Murphy	25	2,275
3.	Kelly	22	2,000
4.	O'Brien	16.5	1,502
5.	O'Connor	15.5	1,410
6.	Ryan	15	1,365
6.	Doyle	15	1,365
8.	Walsh	14.5	1,320
9.	O'Neill	12	1,092
10.	O'Reilly	11.25	1,024
11.	Murray	10.25	932
11.	Dunne	10.25	932
13.	O'Sullivan	9.5	865
14.	Kavanagh	9.33	850
15.	Nolan	9	819
16.	Brennan	8.75	797
17.	Lynch	8.25	752
17.	Kennedy	8.25	752
19.	McCarthy	8	728

20.	Farrell	7.75	706
21.	Carroll	7	637
23.	Daly	6.66	606
24.	Kenny	6.5	600
25.	Fitzpatrick	6.33	576

Names which just miss out on this list are: Fitzgerald, Connolly, McDonnell, Flynn, Duffy, O'Connell, Keogh and Gallagher.

This list represents over 91 pages of the Directory, which means that these 25 surnames occupy just over 8% of all entries in the Directory.

25 most common surnames in Part II Telephone Directory (1984) (measured in columns taken up, with alterations for longer names, marked by an asterisk*)

1.	Murphy	55.5	4,717
2.	O'Connor	45.5	3,868
3.	Ryan	33.5	2,847
4.	O'Brien	33	2,800
5.	Kelly	31.5	2,677
5.	Walsh	31.5	2,677
7.	O'Sullivan	35*	2,650
8.	McCarthy	29.5*	2,234
9.	Byrne	18.5	1,573
10.	O'Neill	18	1,531
11.	Lynch	17	1,445

11.	O'Connell	17	1,445
11.	Fitzgerald	17	1,445
14.	Doyle	14.75	1,254
15.	Collins	13	1,105
15.	O'Leary	13	1,105
15.	Brennan	13	1,105
15.	Daly	13	1,105
19.	O'Shea	12.75	1,096
20.	O'Mahony	13.5*	1,070
21.	O'Donovan	13*	1,062
22.	O'Reilly	11.75	1,051
23.	O'Donnell	11.5	1,040
24.	O'Keeffe	11.25	1,000
25.	Nolan	10	850

*These names, being longer, tend to provide fewer actual surnames for each column, and have been adjusted accordingly.

Exotic North

Most common surnames in Northern Ireland

These are the 25 surnames which appear most often in the Northern Ireland Telephone Directory (1988)

1.	Wilson	2,500 (approx)	5.	Kelly	2,095
1.	Johnston	2,500	6.	Moore	1,920
3.	Campbell	2,300	7.	Browne	1,888
4.	Thompson	2,185	8.	Smyth	1,810

9.	Stewart	1,780	18.	Quinn	1,260
10.	Graham	1,770	19.	Boyd	1,240
11.	Robinson	1,620	20.	Murray	1,190
12.	Hamilton	1,545	21.	Anderson	1,150
12.	O'Neill	1,545	22.	Patterson	1,140
14.	Martin	1,475	22.	Doherty	1,140
15.	Bell	1,357	24.	Clarke	1,120
16.	Murphy	1,300	25.	Hughes	1,090
16.	Scott	1,300			

Among those surnames just barely out of the top 25 are: McLaughlin, Reid, Allen, Donnelly, Ferguson, Kennedy, McCann and Smith.

Note that Kelly is the only surname in Northern Ireland's 10 most common surnames to appear in the Republic of Ireland's top 10.

The most common surnames in each of the counties in Northern Ireland, according to *Irish Family Names,* are:

Antrim	:	Smith
Armagh	:	Murphy
Derry	:	O'Doherty
Down	:	Thompson
Fermanagh	:	Maguire
Tyrone	:	Quinn

Renaming
Old derogatory expressions about Ireland and the Irish

Fair maid of Ireland	Ignis fatuus
Get your Irish up	Lose your temper
Irish apricot	A potato
Irish arms	Thick legs
Irish battleship	A barge
Irish beauty	A woman with 2 black eyes
Irish bridge	A concrete river bed
Irish compliment	A back-handed compliment
Irish confetti	Bricks, especially those thrown in a fight
Irish draperies	Cobwebs
Irish evidence	False evidence
Irish fan	A shovel
Irish grape	A potato
Irish guinea-man	A ship full of emigrants
Irish harp	A long-handled shovel
Irish horse	Corned beef
Irish hurricane	A flat calm with drizzling rain
Irish jig	(rhyming slang) A wig
Irish mail	A toy handcar
Irish nightingale	A tenor
Irish pennants	Fag ends of ropes

Irish rifle	A small comb
Irish root	A penis
Irish rose	(rhyming slang) The nose
Irish theatre	A guard room
Irish toothache	A pregnancy
Irish toyle	A thief with the semblance of a pedlar
Irish turkey	Corned beef and cabbage
Irish wedding	The emptying of a cesspool
Irish whist	Sexual intercourse
Irishman's coat of arms	A black eye
Irishman's dinner	A fast
Irishman's harvest	The Orange season
Irishman's promotion	A reduction in wages, or in position

SAINTS AND SCHOLARS

Amazing grace
9 Irish patron saints

1. St Brigid (Bríde)
   Ireland's second patron saint. Traditionally held to have been born in Co Louth at the time of St Patrick, she is the patron saint of scholars, and also of dairy workers.

2. St Cathal
   A monk from Lismore who lived *circa* AD 85, and became Bishop of Taranto in Italy, he is the patron saint of hernia sufferers.

3. St Columba
   After St Patrick and St Brigid, he is Ireland's third patron saint.

4. St Dunchad
   A saint whose feast day is on 24 May, he is the Irish patron saint of sailors.

5. St Dympna
   A martyr from *circa* AD 650, she is the patron saint of
   a) Mental illness
   b) Epilepsy
   c) Those possessed by the devil
   d) Sleepwalkers

6. St Fiacra
   Born in Ireland *circa* AD 670, he is the patron saint of
   a) Gardeners and horticulturists
   b) Sufferers of venereal diseases and haemorrhoids
   c) Cab and taxi-drivers

7. St Gall
   Born *circa* AD 535, he is the patron saint of birds.

8. St Oliver Plunkett
   Died AD 1681. He is the patron saint of Urban University in Rome.

9. St Patrick
   The principal patron saint of Ireland. Also, on 11 November 1961, he was made secondary patron saint of Nigeria, next only to the Virgin Mary.

The '12 Irish Apostles'

These 12 Irish saints were allegedly trained by St Finnian at Clonard, and were given the collective nickname of the 12 Irish Apostles:

1. St Brendan of Birr	7. St Colum of Tir na nGlas
2. St Brendan of Clonfert	8. St Mobhi of Glasnevin
3. St Canice	9. St Molaise of Deveneish
4. St Ciaran of Saighir	10. St Ninnid of Inismacsaint
5. St Ciaran of Clonmacnoise	11. St Ruadan of Lorrha
6. St Columba	12. St Sinell of Cleenish

Seers
The 3 tragic stories of the Irish

1. *The Death of the Children of Tourau*
2. *The Death of the Children of Lir*
3. *The Death of the Children of Usnach*

The 4 Kerry Poets
A collective name for 4 famous seventeenth- and eighteenth-century Irish poets born in Kerry

1. Pierce Ferriter, hanged in Killarney in 1653

2. Geoffrey O'Donoghue, died in Kerry c. 1685

3. Aodhagan O'Rathaille, died in Kerry 1728

4. Eoghan Rua O Ruilleabhain, died in Kerry 1784

The Irish 5
These are the names of 5 Irish doctors who helped to look after Napoleon while he was in exile on St Helena.

1. Barry Edward O'Meara

2. James Verling

3. Walter Henry

4. George Henry Ruttledge

5. Francis Burton

Fall from grace
Irish people who lost their vocation

1. JEREMIAH CALLANAN (1796–1829)
   The Cork poet went to Maynooth College, followed by Trinity College Dublin, with every intention of becoming a priest. However, on leaving Trinity, he joined the army. He was later to become a tutor, and never entered the service of God.

2. WILLIAM CARLETON (1794–1869)
   The Tyrone-born novelist, as a young man yearned for a life in the priesthood. In 1818, however, he went to Dublin, where he lived in poor circumstances. When offered a commission to write stories showing the superstitions which the Roman Catholic Church allegedly encouraged among the peasantry, he jumped at the chance, and thereafter his attitude to the religion of his upbringing changed dramatically.

3. JOHN BLAKE DILLON (1816–1866)
   The Young Irelander from Ballaghadereen, lawyer, and father of the land agitator John Dillon, having been educated in Maynooth, was intended for the priesthood, but, instead, was called to the Bar in 1841.

4. AUGUSTUS KEANE (1833–1912)
   The Cork-born anthropologist who registered and classified almost every language then known, was originally educated in Dublin and Rome for the Roman Catholic priesthood, but when the time came he refused to enter the Church. He devoted all his life to ethnology.

5. SIR RICHARD MORRISON (1767–1849)
   The architect, chiefly of courthouses and churches throughout Ireland, was intended by his family to take orders. He himself, however, was not keen, and eventually took to learning his trade under James Gandon, thus foregoing his vocation.

6. SEAN O COILEAIN (1756–1816)

The 'Silver Tongue of Munster', poet, became a school-master at Myross in Carbery, Co Cork, rather than take up the vocation intended for him in the priesthood. His chosen profession was not much to his liking either, however, and he became so bitter that his wife left him, and after taking up with her sister, he drove his 'second wife' to such distraction that she burned down his house.

7. LIAM O'FLAHERTY (1897–1984)

The writer was born in the Aran Islands and brought up in a strong Catholic community and family atmosphere. When a priest of the Holy Ghost order managed to persuade him that the priesthood was for him, and when he also agreed to sponsor his education, all looked set for a life of piety for Liam. Having attended Rockwell and Blackrock Colleges, he went to UCD. However he soon discovered that he had no vocation, and not without bad reactions all round, left university, and went to join the British Army.

8. FRANCIS O'NEILL (1849–1936)

The Cork-born Chief of Police in Chicago (1901–1905) had an adventurous early life. Instead of joining the Irish Christian Brothers, he ran away to sea in 1865, at the age of 16. For 4 years he plied the seas eventually getting shipwrecked on Baker's Island in the middle of the Pacific Ocean. He later became Chief of Police in Chicago, but it is as a collector of Irish folk music and dance music that he is best remembered.

9. CAPTAIN MAYNE REID (1818–1883)

The Ballyroney, Co Down-born writer of boys' stories, and adventurer, was originally intended for the Presbyterian ministry by his family. He emigrated, however, to New Orleans, and served in the United States Army during the 1847 Mexican War. He travelled extensively throughout America, and was able to put his first-hand knowledge to touch with over 90 boys' stories, such as 'The Quadroon', 'Scalp Hunters' and 'The Boy Hunters'.

Conversions
Noted Irish people who changed their religion

1. DR THOMAS BARNARDO (1845–1905)
   Founder and director of homes for destitute children,
   whose father was a German furrier of Spanish descent,
   and a devout Catholic, experienced conversion during
   the Protestant religious revival in Dublin in 1862, when he
   was 17.

2. STOPFORD BROOKE (1832–1916)
   Glendowan, Co Derry-born cleric and man of letters; left
   the Church of England in 1880, finding it impossible to
   reconcile his broad Church views with his continuing
   ministry, being Chaplain-in-Ordinary to Queen Victoria.

3. ROGER CASEMENT (1864–1916)
   Irish republican and civil servant; became a Catholic
   days before he was hanged for treason at Pentonville
   prison, in August 1916.

4. WILLIAM CARLETON (1794–1869)
   Writer; was brought up a Catholic and for a time had
   hoped to become a priest. However, he met and fell in
   love with a Protestant girl, Jane Anderson, a niece of 'Fox
   the Proselytiser', and after marrying her, he also became
   a Protestant.

5. AUBREY DE VERE (1814–1902)
   Poet; was born into a traditional Protestant family at
   Curragh Close, Co Limerick. Later, while mixing with
   poets such as Wordsworth, Coleridge and Tennyson, his
   sympathies were strongly drawn to Ireland, and through a
   close friendship with John Henry Newman, he became a
   Catholic at the age of 37, in 1851. His work then became
   that of devotional hymns and the like.

6. REX INGRAM (1893–1950)
   Irish-born Hollywood film director; became a convert to
   Islam.

7. JOSHUA JACOB (1805–1877)

Clonmel-born founder of the White Quakers; abrogated his set later in life after the death of his wife Abigail. He had married a Catholic, gave up his revival movement, and even allowed his children to be educated in the Catholic faith.

8. MAUD GONNE MacBRIDE (1865–1953)

Became a Catholic shortly before she married Major John MacBride in 1903, although she was brought up a Protestant.

9. COUNTESS CONSTANCE MARKIEVICZ (1868–1927)

Irish republican; became a Catholic shortly after her sentence to death for her role in the 1916 Rising, was commuted.

10. GEORGE AUGUSTUS MOORE (1852–1933)

Irish dramatist; brought up as a Catholic. However, he converted to Protestantism later in life, a decision which earned him some notoriety in his native Ireland.

11. ANNIE SMITHSON (1873–1948)

Writer and MP; born into a Protestant family, but, after an unhappy love affair, became a Catholic.

12. JOHN MILLINGTON SYNGE (1871–1909)

Playwright; brought up by his mother, the daughter of an Anglican rector from Co Antrim, in accordance with strict Protestant principles. He gradually renounced Christianity, having read Darwin's *Origin of the Species* when he was fourteen.

13. JOHN TOLAND (1670–1722)

Deistical writer, born of Catholic parents, at Redcastle, Derry. He converted to Protestantism at the age of 16. At the age of 26, he published *Christianity not Mysterious,* in which he maintained that the value of religion could not lie in any unintelligible element, and that no part of the truth could be contrary to reason. This work created a wild uproar, was burned in Ireland by the hangman, and forced him to seek refuge in England.

14. OSCAR WILDE (1854–1900)
Writer and wit who had spent his life debating whether to become a Catholic, finally succumbed to the desire on the day he died. His friend Robert Ross called a Father Cuthbert Dunne to his bedside, and the priest gave him conditional baptism.

12. PEG WOFFINGTON (c. 1714–1760)
Eighteenth-century Irish actress, notorious for her sketchy morals, changed from Catholicism to Protestantism. Later in life, she devoted her time to charity and good works.

Inventors
Noted Irish inventors and their inventions

1. LOUIS BRENNAN (1852–1932)
Mechanical engineer, born in Castlebar, emigrated to Melbourne, Australia, and was working as a watchmaker, when he invented a dirigible torpedo for coastal defence. His patent for a torpedo was purchased by the British government for in excess of £100,000, and Brennan supervised its manufacture, 1887–1896. He was awarded a Companion of Bath in 1892, and later worked on helicopters for the British air ministry 1919–1926. He also invented a gyrostat monorail.

2. ROGER BRESNIHAN
Born in Tralee, Co Kerry in 1881, later to become one of the most famous baseball players of his time in the United States, invented the shin-guard and first put it into use in 1907.

3. LUCIEN BULL
Born in Dublin 1876, invented the electrocardiogram which, by giving a graphic recording of the electrical activity of the heart, is a major tool in assessing heart function.

4. NICHOLAS CALLAN
   Irish priest born in Dublin in 1799, invented the induction coil, a device which led to the modern transformer. It produces electric currents by the process of induction. It consists normally of a soft-iron core, surrounded by a coil of wire, which in turn is surrounded by a second and usually much longer coil. When the current in the inner coil is interrupted, a current much higher than the original one is induced in the outer coil.

5. CHARLES CLIGGET (1740–1795)
   Waterford-born musician, invented a double guitar of 18 strings, and a 'chromatic trumpet and French horn', which anticipated by some 25 years the perfecting of the valve action for brass instruments.

6. AENEAS COFFEY (1797–1840)
   Invented the 'Coffey's Patent Still', which for many years was the standard method for production of industrial spirit. It is recognised as being the first heat exchanger, whose application extended worldwide.

7. MICHAEL CUDAHY
   Co Kilkenny-born, emigrated to the United States, invented a process for meat refrigeration.

8. FRANCIS DANBY (1793–1861)
   Wexford-born landscape and historical painter, noted for his imaginative subjects, was also an accomplished sailor, and invented the 'Danforth' ship's anchor. It is a high-power anchor, designed to reduce weight, and is frequently used for oil rigs.

9. RICHARD EDGEWORTH
   Father of the novelist Maria Edgeworth, spent his whole life inventing things. They include a semaphore, a velocipede and a pedometer.

10. HARRY FERGUSON (1884–1960)
Hillsborough, Co Down-born aviator and inventor, was the first to conceive the revolutionary concept of the tractor and plough designed as one unit. In 1926 he got a patent for the hydraulic regulation of working depth of the various implements of the plough linked with the tractor itself. This invention transformed the face of agriculture.

11. JOHN ROBERT GREGG
Monaghan-born, published in 1888 his *Light-Line Phonography,* later known as the Gregg Shorthand System. A major rival, in particular in the United States, to the Pitman system, its success is based on his employing shorthand characters that were in harmony with the slant and movement of the longhand, the lack of which had given rise to many criticisms of the existing systems.

12. THOMAS GRUBB
Born in Kilkenny in 1800, invented a revolutionary and ingenious machine which advanced printing technology; called a 'bank note printer', it could, for the first time, engrave, print and number bank notes.

13. MICHAEL HICKS
Meath man, invented the 'Hurricane Lamp', in order to aid railway workers. It was designed so as not to be extinguished by violent winds.

14. JOHN HOLLAND (1841–1914)
Born in Liscannor, Co Clare, invented, designed and built the first submarine, which was purchased on 18 April 1900. Called 'The Holland', it had a gasoline engine for surface propulsion and an electric motor fed by storage batteries for power when it was submerged.

15. JOHN JOLY (1857–1933)
Offaly-born engineer, geologist and physicist, invented many things in his fields, including a meldometer, a hydrostatic balance, a steam calorimeter, and a photometer to measure illumination. He was also a pioneer of colour photography.

16. JOHN HOWARD KYAN (1774–1850)
    Born in Dublin, invented, between 1812–1836, the 'Kyanising' process for processing wood. He died in New York.

17. SIR JAMES MARTIN
    Inventor of the 'Aircraft Ejector Seat', was born in Crosscar, Co Down. He developed his device simultaneously with the Germans, and, as it saved the lives of 3,500 pilots during the Second World War, he was knighted by the British.

18. A. H. McGAULEY
    Dubliner, invented, in 1833, what was called a 'Trembler Interrupter', which was the forerunner of the electric bell.

19. ALEXANDER MITCHELL (1780–1868)
    Invented the 'Mitchell Screw Pile', a simple and effective way of constructing lighthouses in deep water, on shifting sands, or on mud patches.

20. RICHARD POCKRICH
    Born in 1690, Co Monaghan, invented musical glasses, also known as harmonically arranged glasses.

21. JOHN ROWAN (1787–1858)
    Linen-spinner born at Doagh, near Ballyclare, Co Antrim, invented a steam-driven vehicle, which was later claimed to be the first motor car.

22. JOE SHERIDAN
    Dublin chef, invented Irish Coffee while working in Foynes in 1943.

23. JOHN WALKER
    From Castlecomer, Co Kilkenny, invented, in 1899, 'Caterpillar Tracks' for tanks and artillery. The first commercially practical one was tested on 24 November 1904.

24. SIR WILLIAM WILDE (1815–1876)
    The Co Roscommon-born husband of the poet 'Speranza' and father of Oscar Wilde, invented the 'Ophthalmoscope', an instrument for inspecting the interior of the eye, especially the retina.

By Any Other Name

Irishmen giving their names to scientific/
medical terms etc.

1. DR BARNARDO'S HOMES
   Started up by the Dublin-born doctor and philanthropist,
   Thomas John Barnardo. Having founded the East End
   juvenile mission for destitute children in London in 1867,
   he went on to open (in 1870), a boys' home in Stepney,
   which developed into the now world-renowned 'Dr
   Barnardo's Homes'. In 1876, Barnardo founded the Girls'
   Village Home at Barkingside in Essex. By the time he died
   in 1905, he had assisted 250,000 children.

2. BEAUFORT'S SCALE
   A series of numbers used by meteorologists to indicate
   force of a wind at sea (measured at 10 metres above the
   ground) was devised by the Dublin-born Admiral Sir
   Francis Beaufort. When he devised the scale, he scaled
   the wind speeds from one to 12, from 'calm' at force 0, to
   force 12, 'that which no canvas could withstand'. The
   system has been much adapted and now reaches a
   maximum of force 17, corresponding to winds 126–136
   mph.

3. BENNETT'S FRACTURE
   Discovered in 1881 by Edward Hallaran Bennett
   (1837–1907), a Cork-born authority on bone fractures.
   Bennett was Professor of Surgery at Trinity College
   Dublin, 1873–1906, and he formed a collection of fract-
   ures at the pathological museum of TCD.

4. BOYLE'S LAW
   One of the major laws of physics is named after the
   natural philosopher and chemist, Robert Boyle
   (1627–1691), who was born at Lismore Castle, at
   Lismore, Co Waterford. The law which Boyle was the first
   to formulate, states that the volume of a given quantity of
   gas varies inversely with the pressure when the
   temperature is constant. Boyle was also one of the
   founders of the Royal Society.

5. THE COLLES FRACTURE
A fracture of the lower end of the radius causing backward and outward displacement of the wrist and hand, is named after the Irish surgeon, Abraham Colles (1773–1843), who first described it in 1814. Later, in his *Practical Observations on the Venereal Disease* (1837), he stated that a child affected with congenital syphilis, whose mother shows no signs of the disease, will not infect her. This is known as Colles' Law.

6. GRAVE'S DISEASE
A medical term for toxic or exophthalmic goitre, it is called after the Dublin-born physician, Robert James Graves (1796–1853). This ailment is characterised by the association of hyperthyroidism, protrusion of the eyes, and a diffuse enlargement of the thyroid. Graves, who was President of the Irish College of Physicians 1843–1844, also made advances in the treatment and feeding of fever victims.

7. JACOB'S ULCER
An eye condition discovered by the Maryborough (Portlaoise)-born Irish oculist, Arthur Jacob (1790–1874). Jacob was Professor of Anatomy at the Royal College of Surgeons of Ireland 1826–1869.

8. THE KELVIN TEMPERATURE SCALE
Also known as the Absolute Temperature scale, it is called after the Belfast-born physicist, William Thomson Kelvin, the 1st Baron Kelvin of Largs. Its 'Absolute Zero' is at -273 degrees Celsius, which is the point at which all molecular motion ceases. Kelvin made major advances in the science of thermodynamics and electricity, he improved the system of electrical units, and also invented several scientific units, including the Kelvin compass, the Kelvin balance, and the Kelvin tide predictor.

9. THE STOKES'-ADAMS SYNDROME
Named after the nineteenth-century Sligo-born mathematician and physicist, Sir George Gabriel Stokes.

Nobel Honours
Ireland's Nobel Prize winners

1. 1923 LITERATURE PRIZE
    Awarded to William Butler Yeats, 'for his always inspired poetry, which in a highly artistic form gives expression to the spirit of a whole nation'.

2. 1925 LITERATURE PRIZE
    Awarded to George Bernard Shaw, 'for his work which is marked by both idealism and humanity, its stimulating satire often being infused with a singular poetic beauty'.

3. 1951 PHYSICS PRIZE
    Awarded to Ernest Thomas Sinton Walton, and the Englishman, Sir John Douglas Cockroft, 'for their pioneer work on the transmutation of atomic nucleii by artificially accelerating atomic particles'.

4. 1969 LITERATURE PRIZE
    Awarded to Samuel Beckett, 'for his writing, which – in new forms for the novel and drama – in the distinction of modern man acquires its elevation'.

5. 1974 PEACE PRIZE
    Awarded to Sean MacBride, for his work as President of the International Peace Bureau, and as the Commissioner of Namibia for the United Nations in New York. He shared the prize with Eisaku Sato, the Prime Minister of Japan.

6. 1976 PEACE PRIZE
    Awarded to Mairead Corrigan and Betty Williams for their founding of the Peace People in Northern Ireland. They received their award in 1977.

Unrequited Love
8 famous Irish marriage refusals

1. JOHN BANIM (1798–1842)
   Writer, co-author with his brother Michael of *Tales of the O'Hara Family*, had his youth darkened by an unhappy love affair. He got engaged to one of the pupils in the drawing class he was teaching in Kilkenny. She later broke it off, and died soon after. This shattered Banim, and although he married later on, his health never recovered from the shock and he died aged 46.

2. MARIA EDGEWORTH (1767–1849)
   Was proposed to by a Swedish gentleman, M. Edelcranz. She liked him immensely, but out of duty to her family and her father, had to turn him down. This conflict of duty over feelings is a common thread throughout her many works.

3. EDEL MARY QUINN (1907–1944)
   The Legion of Mary envoy in Africa, preferring to enter a contemplative order, refused a proposal of marriage in 1927 from the young Frenchman for whom she was working as a secretary.

4. JONATHAN SWIFT (1667–1745)
   Proposed marriage to the sister of a friend of his. But, apparently because of his poverty, Jane Waring (whom Swift had nicknamed Varina), scorned his proposal. Swift took this very philosophically, and when he later became famous, she tried to redress what she now saw as a major error on her part. He wrote her a nasty reply, to which he never received an answer.

5.   JOHN MILLINGTON SYNGE (1871–1909)
The playwright proposed twice to a woman called Cherrie
Matheson, when he was 24, and again in 1899, when he
was 25. Although she was deeply devoted to him, she
was a devout member of the Plymouth Brethren, and as
she could not marry a non-believer, she had on both
occasions to turn him down. Synge is also reputed to
have asked, in vain, the hand in marriage of two different
girl students in Paris.

6.   OSCAR WILDE (1856–1900)
Proposed marriage to Charlotte Montefiore in either 1880
or 1881. When she turned him down, he wrote her a note
saying 'Charlotte, I am so sorry about your decision. With
your money and my brain we could have gone so far.' He
had previously proposed to a Florence Balcombe, and
earlier still had contemplated marrying a Violet Hunt. He
eventually married Constance Lloyd on 29 May 1884.

7.   W.B. YEATS (1865–1939)
The poet met Maud Gonne in 1890 through the Fenian,
John O'Leary. He fell madly in love with her, but in 1891,
when he proposed marriage to her, she turned him down.
She was to turn him down a number of times again in the
future. Yeats also unsuccessfully proposed to her
daughter Iseult Gonne.

8.   PEG WOFFINGTON (1720–1760)
The actress, whose beauty and coquetry carried many a
heart by storm, met David Garrick in 1742, when she
played Cordelia to his King Lear in London. Having
become lovers, and set up home together, they agreed to
marry. But her abrasiveness along with his parsimony
caused them to drift apart in 1744.

Singles
Famous Irish people who never married

1. William Archer, first librarian of the National Library

2. George Benn, Belfast historian

3. Joseph Biggar (1828–1890), nationalist politician

4. James Bourchier (1850–1920), *Times* correspondent in the Balkans

5. Sir Frederick Burton (1816–1900), water-colour painter

6. William Congreve (1670–1729), novelist

7. Daniel Corkery (1878–1964), writer

8. Thomas Davis (1814–1845), poet and patriot

9. Anne Devlin (c. 1778–1851)

10. Joseph 'Wee Joe' Devlin (1872–1934), nationalist politician

11. John Devoy (1842–1928), Fenian

12. Maria Edgeworth (1767–1849), novelist

13. Barry Fitzgerald (1888–1961), actor

14. George Fitzmaurice (1877–1963), playwright

15. Oliver Goldsmith (1728–1774), writer

16. Maurice Gorham (1902–1975), RTE director and journalist

17. Sir Joseph Larmor (1841–1942), physicist

18. Sir Thomas Lipton (1850–1931), grocer, tea merchant and yachtsman

19. Francis Magan (1772–1843), informer

20. Narcissus Marsh (1638–1713), librarian

21. Edward Martin (1859–1923), dramatist

22. George Moore (1852–1933), novelist and dramatist

23. George O'Brien (1892–1973), economist

24. John O'Leary (1830–1907), President of IRB 1885–1907

25. Eoin O'Mahony (1904–1970), raconteur and genealogist

26. Sir Horace Plunkett (1854–1932), agriculturalist and Unionist politician

27. Forrest Reid (1876–1947), novelist

28. Edith Somerville (1858–1949), novelist

29. John Millington Synge (1871–1909), playwright

Innocence and Experience
Famous Irish 'young' marriages

1. CHARLES BIANCONI

   The Lombardy-born businessman, who started the first public conveyance between Clonmel and Cahir in 1815, married the beautiful Irish girl, Eliza Hayes, when she was only 18.

2. MARGUERITE, THE COUNTESS OF BLESSINGTON

   The author, who was later to become the lover of Count D'Orsay, was, in 1804, at the age of 14, forced into marrying a worthless Captain Farmer. She quit him in the short space of three months, and in 1818, after Farmer died, married the Earl of Blessington.

3. HENRY BROOKE

   The eighteenth-century author of *The Fool of Quality*, a friend of Swift and Pope, had left Trinity 4 years earlier when, in 1728, at the age of only 20, he married his ward, and cousin, Catherine Meares, when she was either 14 or 15 years old. Brooke went on to father 22 children.

4. SIR JOHN LAVERY

The Belfast-born painter had a daughter about the same age as Hazel Trudeau when, at the age of 55, he married Hazel in 1910. She was 29. Sir John's first wife had died in childbirth, and Hazel Trudeau had also previously been married. She was born in Chicago as Hazel Martyn, in 1881.

5. JUSTIN McCARTHY

Irish politician, historian and novelist, whose work includes *History of Our Times, Dear Lady Disdain* and *Miss Misanthrope,* married an 18-year-old girl when he was 64, in 1894.

6. JUSTIN HUNTLY McCARTHY

Irish Parliamentary party politician, author, and son of the writer Justin McCarthy, married a 17-year-old Glasgow music hall entertainer, Cissie Lawler.

7. JOHN MITCHEL

Famous for his *Jail Journal,* entered a solicitor's office in Newry after leaving Trinity College. From there, in 1836, he eloped to England with 16-year-old Jane Verner. The course of true love did not run smooth, as they were brought back to custody in Ireland. However, the following year, when he was 22 and Jane was just 17, they eloped again, and married.

8. LOLA MONTEZ

Real name, Marie Dolores Eliza Rosanna Gilbert, the Limerick-born adventuress and 'Spanish' dancer who achieved international notoriety through her association with King Ludwig I of Bavaria, was only 15 years old when she married a Captain Thomas James. But as he was very cruel to her, the marriage soon broke up.

9. EIBHLIN DHUBH NI CONAILL

Penned the famous lament for her dead husband, *Caoineadh Airt Ui Laoighaire;* forced by her mother, at a very young age (of perhaps 15), to marry an elderly man, O'Connor of Iveragh. He died 6 months later, and she then went off, against the wishes of her family, to elope with O'Leary.

10. GRACE O'MALLEY

Legendary pirate queen of Clare Island, thought to have been only 15 years old when she married Donal O'Flaherty in 1546. He was a member of a prominent pirating family, and was later killed in battle.

11. THOMAS MOORE

The poet and composer, was 30 years old when, in March 1811, he married a 16-year-old Irish actress, Elizabeth 'Betsy' Dyke. Her actual age is not certain, and estimates range from 14 to 18 years. She lived till 1867, surviving her husband and their 5 children.

12. RICHARD BRINSLEY SHERIDAN

The playwright met Elizabeth Anne Linley in 1771 when, as the eldest daughter of the composer, Thomas Linley, the 16-year-old was an up and coming oratorio singer, and the prima donna of her father's concerts. Exceedingly beautiful (her portrait, by Gainsborough, hangs at Knole, Kent), she was not yet 18 when Sheridan, in order to steal a march on her many suitors, married her secretly near Calais in March 1772, when Sheridan himself was just 21.

13. THEOBALD WOLFE TONE

The man who later helped found the United Irishmen was 22 years of age when he married Matilda Witherington, a 15-year-old girl, with whom he had eloped when still at Trinity College, in 1885.

Gluttons for Punishment
Famous Irish people who married twice (at least)

1. MOLLY ALLGOOD (1887–1952)
   In 1911 the actress married the drama critic of the *Manchester Herald,* George Herbert Mair, just over 2 years after the death of her fiancé John Millington Synge. She was 24. Herbert died after 15 years of marriage and 2 children. After only 6 months, Molly remarried, this time to Abbey actor, Arthur Sinclair. This ended in divorce difficulties.

2. TODD ANDREWS (1901–1985)
   The founder of Bord na Mona lost his first wife, Mary Coyle (by whom he had 5 children, 2 of them becoming TDs), when he was 66. He then married Joyce Duffy, who survived him when he died in 1985.

3. JOHN C. BERESFORD (1738–1805)
   The Dublin-born statesman, who had extraordinary influence on eighteenth-century Ireland, lost his first wife when he was 36. Two years later, in 1774, he married Barbara Montgomery, a much-vaunted beauty who was celebrated by the painter Sir Joshua Reynolds who made her one of his 'Graces'.

4. DION BOUCICAULT (1820–1890)
   The playwright married 3 times, and was bigamously married to his third wife.

5. THE COUNTESS OF BLESSINGTON, MARGUERITE POWER (1789–1849)
   She was released from a very unhappy first marriage to a Captain Farmer, when in 1817, he was killed in a drunken brawl. A few months later, she married the Earl of Blessington. A renowned beauty, she lived 20 years after the death of the Earl, and died at the age of 60.

6. VISCOUNT CASTLEROSSE, VALENTINE BROWNE (1891–1943)
   The columnist and founder of Killarney Golf Club married Doris Delavigne in 1926, when he was 35. Although they divorced in 1938, he did not remarry until 3 weeks after her death in 1942. However he died a year after this marriage with the Australian widow, Lady Enid Furness.

7. PATRICK CAMPBELL (1913–1980)
   The Dublin-born writer, broadcaster, and long-time guest on the TV show *Call My Bluff* on BBC, married Sylvia Willoughby Lee in 1941. It was dissolved after 6 years, soon after which he married Cherry Louise Munro. In 1966 that marriage was also dissolved, and in November of the same year, at the age of 53, he married an ex-film script writer and producer, Vivienne Orme.

8. ERSKINE CHILDERS (1905–1974)
   The fourth President of Ireland married Ruth Ellen Dow in 1925, and had 2 sons and 3 daughters by this union. She died in 1950, and in 1952 he remarried Rita Dudley, by whom he had another daughter, Nessa.

9. CON CREMIN (1908–1987)
   The diplomat, having lost his first wife, remarried when he was 71 years of age, in 1979.

10. RICHARD CROKER (1841–1922)
    The Clonakilty-born 'Boss' of Tammany Hall in New York, lost his first wife in 1914, when he was 73. He created a controversy, and got involved in litigation with his family, when he went on to marry a Cherokee Indian, Bewla Benton Edmundson, from Oklahoma.

11. CYRIL CUSACK
    Ireland's premier actor of stage and screen married an actress, Margaret Kiely, by whom his 4 actress daughters were born. When she died, he met his second wife, Mary, during the making of the film, *The Taming of the Shrew.*

12. CHRISTIAN DAVIES
    The amazing Irish woman soldier (1637–1739), married a waiter, Richard Welsh, from the inn that she had inherited,

when she was 21. Later, after he had been pressed to fight in Flanders, she spent 13 years looking for him. They were reunited for 3 years, after which he was killed in battle. She then married a grenadier, Hugh Jones, but he was also killed in battle. Finally, after returning to Dublin, she married yet another soldier. She died in obscurity in Chelsea, at the age of 62.

13. FRANK HARRIS (1856–1931)
The adventurer and writer, married when he was 31, a rich widow, Mary Clayton, but it soon failed. In 1894 he eloped with Helen O'Hara, and went on to marry her. His autobiography, published in 5 volumes between 1923 and 1927, details his self-proclaimed sexual prowess.

14. LOLA MONTEZ (1818–1861)
The Limerick-born dancer, despite living to the age of only 43, was married 3 times. Her first marriage, to a Captain James, ended in divorce after 5 years. In 1849, when she was 31, she married a Lieutenant Heald. He died soon after. Then, at the age of 35, she married for a third time, to a San Francisco man, P.P. Hull. This ended in divorce.

15. EARL NUGENT (1702–1788)
The poet-politician was so adept at marrying rich widows that Robert Walpole named this practice 'Nugentising' in his honour. His 3 marriages, to the daughter of the Earl of Fingal, to Anne Knight, and to the widow of the 4th Earl of Berkeley, all augmented his wealth.

16. GRACE O'MALLEY
The 'Queen' of Clare Island was married twice, firstly to one of the O'Flaherty clan, and then in 1582 to the Chief of the Burkes of Mayo, Richard Burke.

17. MARIE LOUISE O'MORPHI (1736–1815)
The Irish courtesan in the France of Louis XV married 3 times. Her first marriage was arranged by Madame Pompadour, to an ageing army officer. When he was killed in battle in 1757, she married a court official. When he too died in 1790, she married a Monsieur Dumont, a revolutionary, who was 20 years younger than Marie-Louise.

18. MELASINA TRENCH (1768–1827)
    The Dublin-born author, married a Colonel St George when she was 16. He died 2 years later. She went on to marry a Richard Trench, from Moate, Co Westmeath in 1803.

19. TWICE IN ONE DAY
    In 1938, in the village of Killeter near Newtown Stewart in Northern Ireland, a local girl was married by mistake to the taxi driver who brought her to the ceremony. He had possession of the ring, and unwittingly took the place of the groom when it came to putting the ring on the bride's finger. The mistake was discovered when it came to the signing of the registry. The ceremony had to be repeated, so this lass has the unenviable distinction of being wed twice in the same day.

Sires and Dams
Notable Irish people who had large families

22 HENRY BROOKE
   Writer, had family of 22 children, including his daugher Charlotte, who herself became a renowned writer.

21 ARTHUR GUINNESS
   Founder of the Guinness brewery dynasty, had 21 children, only 10 of whom survived infancy.

18 NAN DONAGHUE
   Subject of Sharon Gmelch's biography, *The Life of an Irish Travelling Woman,* had 18 children, 4 by her first husband Jim Browne, and 14 with Mick Donaghue. She herself was one of 11 children.

16 MARTIN CREGAN
   Landscape painter, had 16 children.

15 DOROTHY JORDAN
   Late eighteenth- early nineteenth-century actress, bore 15 children, by 3 different men.

13 MAURICE SHEEHY
    Former MD of the Sugar Company, has with his wife Cathleen, 9 sons and 4 daughters.

12 MATT LYONS
    The meat baron, has a family of 12 children, 7 sons and 5 daughters.

    DENIS GALLAGHER
    Fianna Fail TD for Mayo West, and former government minister, and his wife Hannah, have 5 sons and 7 daughters.

    CHRISSIE WARD
    A founder of the traveller's rights group, Minceir Misli, has 12 children.

11 ANTHONY WEST
    Co Down-born author, has 11 children.

10 PEIG SAYERS
    'Queen of the Storytellers', herself one of a family of 13, had 10 of her own children.

    ABRAHAM COLLES
    Irish doctor after whom the 'Colles Fracture' is named, had 10 children.

    TOMMY DOYLE
    Legendary Tipperary hurler, and his wife Nancy, have had 10 children.

    EUGENE LAMBERT
    Famed puppeteer, has a family of 10.

    PADDY POWER
    Fianna Fail TD for Kildare, and former government minister and MEP, has 10 children, 7 sons and 3 daughters. He married Kitty Martin in 1955.

    TOMAS O'CRIOMHTHAIN
    Fisherman and writer of *An tOileanach,* reared 10 children on the Blaskets.

CORMAC BRESLIN
Donegal Fianna Fail TD 1937–1973 and ex-Ceann
Comhairle, and his wife Antoinette, have had 8 sons and
2 daughters.

9   CHARLES GALLAGHER
Builder and chairman of the Abbey Group, had 9
children.

Family Power
Notable Irish people who came from large families

---

24   LARRY DUNNE: most infamous of an infamous Dublin
family, is one of 24 children of 'Bronco' Dunne.

23   PECKER DUNNE: tinker ballad singer, was one of 21 out
of 23 children who survived into adulthood.

22   EIBHLIN DHUBH NI CHONAILL: wrote the famous lament
to her husband, *Caoineadh Airt Ui Laoghaire,* was one of
22 children of Domhnaill Mor O'Connaill, the grandfather
of Daniel O'Connell.

MARIA EDGEWORTH: novelist, was the third oldest of 22
children, only 19 of whom survived infancy.

21   CHRISTY BROWN: disabled Irish writer, was one of only
11 of his mother's children to survive into adulthood.

19   ANNA HASLAM: suffragist, who lived until the age of 93,
was one of 19 children.

17   DAN DONNELLY: prize fighter, was the ninth out of 17
children, in which there were 4 sets of twins.

16   SIR JONAH BARRINGTON: politician, judge and author,
was the fourth of 16 children.

LILIAN BEHAN: British Ladies Amateur Golf Champion
1985, only the sixth Irish woman to achieve this feat, is
the tenth oldest of a family of 16.

CARDINAL PAUL CULLEN: Ballitore, Co Kildare-born first Irish Cardinal, was one of 16 offspring.

15   RICHARD ALLEN: Quaker, philanthropist, world traveller, and draper, was the fourth eldest of 15 children.

JAMES JOYCE: writer, was the oldest of 15 children, only 10 of whom survived infancy.

14   ROBERT BOYLE: discoverer of Boyle's Law, was the seventh son, and the 14th child of the great Earl of Cork.

WILLIAM CARLETON: writer, was the youngest of 14 children, his parents had only 14 acres of land to disperse among them.

CHARLES GALLAGHER: Abbey Chairman, is the youngest of 14.

DAN SPRING: father of Dick and Donal Spring, who spent 39 years in the Oireachtas, was one of 14 children.

13   JOSHUA BEWLEY: founder of Bewley's, was the youngest of 13 children, his mother being 48 when he was born.

JOHN FORD: Irish-American film director, was the 13th and youngest of a large family.

LADY DOROTHY LOWRY-CORRY: Fermanagh-born archaeologist, was one of 13.

SEAN O'CASEY: the playwright was the youngest of 13 children in a poor family, and only 5 survived childhood.

KITTY O'SHEA: lover and later wife of Charles Stewart Parnell, was the youngest of 13 children.

PEIG SAYERS: writer, was one of only 4 children of the 13 her mother bore to survive childhood.

12   NED CASH: 'King of the Horse Dealers', was from a family of 12.

MARTIN DEMPSEY: actor and comedian, was the last of 12 children.

NOEL DEMPSEY: Fianna Fail TD for Meath, is one of 12 sons.

LORD EDWARD FITZGERALD: the United Irishman of the 1798 rebellion, was the 12th child of the 20th Earl of Kildare.

THOMAS MacCURTAIN: first Republican Lord Mayor of Cork, was the youngest in a family of 12.

JIMMY McLARNIN: Irish-born world boxing champion, was one of a dozen children.

MOTHER MARY MARTIN: foundress of the Medical Missionaries of Mary, was the eldest of 12 children of a Dublin timber merchant.

BRIAN O'NOLAN (MYLES na gCOPALEEN): the third eldest of 12 children.

NOEL PEARSON: impresario, was the fifth eldest of 8 sons and 4 daughters.

MATT TALBOT: reformed alcoholic, was the second eldest of 12 children of Charles Talbot, a labourer with the Port and Docks Board.

11 LARRY COYNE: Kinnegad-born head of Film Four International at Channel Four TV, was one of 11 children.

HARRY FERGUSON: aviator and inventor, was the fourth son in a family of 11 children.

JOE FOYLE: speed reading tutor, was the 9th child in an 11-boy family.

COUNT JOHN McCORMACK: world-renowned tenor, was the fourth in a line of 11 children, only 5 of whom survived childhood.

PATRICK MacGILL: author, was the oldest of 11 offspring of a small farmer in Glenties, Co Donegal

10 EDWARD (NED) DALY: one of the 16 men executed after the Easter Rising of 1916, was the only boy in a family of 10.

ALICE GLENN: controversial politician, is the eldest of 10 children.

NAN JOYCE: traveller, was one of 10 children.

TOM MURPHY: the playwright, is the youngest of 10 children.

HELEN WADDELL: writer, was the youngest of 10 children of a Presbyterian clergyman from Glenarm, Co Antrim.

9 SARAH CURRAN: lover of Robert Emmet, was the youngest of 9.

PADDY 'THE COPE' GALLAGHER: the co-operative pioneer, was the eldest of 9 children.

SEAMUS HEANEY: the poet, is the eldest of 9 children.

JIMMY INGLE: European boxing champion, had eight brothers, all of whom also boxed.

DONAL LUNNY: musician, is one of 9 children.

BRIAN MOORE: Belfast-born novelist, is the fourth eldest in a family of 9.

LIAM O'FLAHERTY: writer, was the second son in a family of at least 9 children.

An Only Child
Some names of those who grew up as an only child

Pat Bolger: agricultural writer and humorist

Elizabeth Bowen: novelist

Bob Carlile: actor, singer, and accountant

Brendan Crinion: former Meath TD and farmer

Olga Pyne Clarke: writer

Pan Collins: ex-*Late Late Show* researcher (and her husband, Kevin)

Gerard Connolly: former Offaly TD

Cyril Cusack: actor

John de Courcy Ireland: writer on naval matters

Aidan Grennell: actor

Bill Harpur: RTE film expert

John Feeney: ex-*Evening Herald* journalist

Tom Johnson: first leader of the parliamentary Labour Party

Denis Johnston: writer and playwright

Paddy Lalor: MEP

Mary Lavin: writer

Sir Thomas Lipton: tea merchant and yachtsman

Maire McSweeney Brugha: teacher, and wife of Ruari Brugha

Eamonn Morrissey: actor and comedian

Van Morrison: singer/songwriter

Iris Murdoch: novelist

George O'Brien: historian, writer and Senator

Donnacha O'Dea: swimmer and gambler

Twink (Adele King): actress and singer

Dermot Weld: horse trainer

Andrew Whitaker: motoring correspondent

John O'Donoghue: TV presenter

Patrick Riddell: writer and playwright

Patrick Stevenson: artist

True Grit
Irish people who triumphed over handicap

1. SIR ROBERT BALL (1840–1913)
   Irish astronomer so dedicated to his work, and observing through telescopes to such an extent, that his right eye became impaired in 1883. The eye had to be removed altogether in 1897. Despite this obvious handicap he was able to continue to hold the chair of Astronomy at Cambridge until his death. He was elected president of the Royal Astronomical Society and of the Mathematical Association.

2. 'BILLY THE BOWL'
   Eighteenth-century beggar, became a robber, and eventually resorted to murder. He managed all his exploits despite having been born without legs. His nickname came from the fact that he propelled himself around in a large wooden bowl protected by iron bands. He was eventually apprehended in 1786.

3. CHRISTY BROWN (1932–1981)
   Dublin writer almost completely paralysed by a variety of Cerebral Palsy. Overcame his handicap with the help of his mother, when he learned to write with a pencil between the toes of his left foot. He is best known for the novel *Down All the Days,* and the autobiographical *My Left Foot.*

4. FRANCES BROWNE (1816–1879)
   The 'Blind Poetess of Donegal', contracted smallpox as an infant, and became totally blind. In spite of this she published, among many works, the world best-seller, *Granny's Wonderful Chair and the Stories It Told.*

5. CATHAL BRUGHA (1874–1922)
   Republican soldier and Sinn Fein politician, crippled permanently as a result of wounds received in action while second-in-command to Eamonn Ceannt at the South Dublin Union garrison, in the Easter Rising of 1916.

However, he was elected President of the Assembly of the first Dail in 1919, and held the post of Minister for National Defence until his death, in heroic circumstances, in 1922.

6. SIR FREDERICK BURTON (1816–1900)
   Corofin-born Irish watercolour artist and portrait painter, made it to the top of his profession despite losing all ability in his right arm when he was a child, as a result of an accident. He became a member of the Royal Hibernian Academy in 1839, was Director of London's National Gallery for 20 years, and painted the portraits of such celebrities as Thomas Davis, Eugene O'Curry and Samuel Ferguson.

7. FATHER LEO CLOSE (1934–1977)
   Paralysed at 21, rendered immobile from the chest downwards. Went on to found the Irish and New Zealand Wheelchair Associations, and also won Gold medals in Paraplegic Olympics.

8. MICHAEL DAVITT (1846–1906)
   Land reformer, born into a poor Catholic family in Straide, Co Mayo, and after the Famine emigrated to Haslingden in Lancashire, where he sought work in a local cotton mill in 1856, at the age of 10. Not long after, at the age of 11, he caught his right arm in a machine in the mill, which resulted in it being amputated. Despite this setback, he went on to become one of Ireland's best known revolutionaries and land agitators.

9. ST JOHN ERVINE (1883–1971)
   Belfast-born playwright, critic and novelist, lost a leg when serving in the First World War with the Dublin Fusiliers. He later became an influential drama critic with papers such as the *Observer,* and wrote a number of well-received plays and novels. He lived until the ripe old age of 88.

10. CARL HARDBECK (1869–1945)
    German-born musician and collector of traditional Irish music, blind from birth. However he trained as an organist, pianist and music teacher, and went on to invent a Gaelic Braille. He worked in Belfast and throughout the

Irish Gaeltacht and became Professor of Music at UCC. His contribution to Irish music, despite his lack of sight, was enormous.

11. PAUL HENRY (1876–1958)
Belfast-born artist whose work is still highly regarded and much sought after by collectors, totally blind for the last 13 years of his creative life. In fact, a red-green colour blindness was his from birth, but neither of these handicaps stopped him painting his distinctive landscapes of both Achill and Connemara.

12. CHARLES KICKHAM (1828–1882)
Tipperary-born author and Fenian, involved in a nasty accident at the age of 13 which greatly impaired his eyesight and vision. Gunpowder exploded in his face from a powder flask. Went on to write such novels as *Knocknagow* and *Sally Cavanagh.*

13. SEAN MacDIARMADA (1884–1916)
One of the 7 signatories of the 1916 Proclamation, stricken in 1912 by an attack of polio which, despite leaving him virtually crippled, did not deter him from his work with the IRB. Executed in 1916 for his role in the Easter Rising.

14. VIOLET MARTIN (1862–1915)
'Ross' half of Somerville and Ross team, most famous for their *Some Experiences of an Irish R.M.,* confined in all her movements as a result of a serious accident at the age of 36. Most of her writings, in close partnership with her cousin and life-long friend, were produced after this life-shortening experience.

15. CHRISTOPHER NOLAN
Born Mullingar, 1965, overcame an accident of birth which left him severely handicapped, and with the help of his mother, he learned to type with a stick attached to his forehead. His *Damburst of Dreams,* published in 1981, won praise, but it was not until 1987 when he won the Whitbread Prize for his *Under the Eye of the Clock,* that he gained world recognition, to the extent that Ronald Reagan called him 'the greatest man alive'.

16. ERNIE O'MALLEY (1898–1957)
    Castlebar-born republican and writer, so badly injured in a raid in Dublin in November 1922, that he was told that he would never walk again. However he made sufficient recovery to visit and/or live in such diverse places as Spain, California, New Mexico, Mexico, New York, and eventually back in Mayo and Dublin.

17. FRANCIS O'NEILL (1849–1936)
    Bantry-born Chicago Chief of Police from 1901 to 1905, renowned collector of Irish dance and folk music. As a raw recruit in the Chicago Police Force at the age of 24, he was shot in the back by a gunman he had encountered. Promoted for his bravery, he lived till the age of 87. For the last 43 years of his life that bullet remained in his back.

18. EDEL QUINN (1907–1943)
    Cork girl, who despite suffering from advanced tuberculosis, spent 13 years working in Africa in the Legion of Mary. A prime example of enduring against the odds. She set up branches for the Legion in Nairobi, Kenya, Uganda, Mauritius and Nyasaland.

19. ANTHONY RAFTERY ('Mise Raftaire an File') (1784–1835)
    Famed Irish poet, known locally in Connacht as 'The Kiltimagh Fiddler', made blind as a child as a result of smallpox. This did not prevent him from becoming a famous wandering bard, particularly throughout the counties of Galway and Mayo.

20. FRANK RYAN (1902–1944)
    Socialist republican, almost stone deaf, yet when he became editor of *An Phoblacht,* it was said of him that he could always hear any offer of money for this paper.

21. MICHAEL MORAN (1794–1846)
    Better known as 'Zozimus', the famous Dublin street balladeer and singer. Was blind from birth. His regular performances on the bridges spanning his beloved Liffey, made him one of the great 'characters' of old Dublin.

Cheating the executioner
Irish people sentenced to be executed, but survived to become …

1.	Lady Betty	Public hangwoman, Roscommon
2.	Thomas Francis Bourke	Council member of the Fenians
3.	Robert Brennan	Minister to the United States 1938–1947
4.	Edward O'Meaher Condon	Allies supporter in First World War
5.	William T. Cosgrave	President of the Executive Council of the Irish Free State, 1923–1933
6.	Eamon de Valera	President of Dail Eireann, 1919–1921; President of the Irish Republic, 1921–1922; President of the Executive Council of the Free State, 1932–1937; Taoiseach, 1937–1948, 1951–1954 and 1957–1959; President of Ireland, 1969–1973
7.	Sir Charles Gavan Duffy	Prime Minister of Victoria
8.	Patrick Donaghue	Brigadier General, United States Army
9.	Richard Hayes	Film Censor, 1944–1954
10.	Michael Ireland	Attorney General of Australia
11.	Morris Lyene	Attorney General of Australia
12.	Sean MacEntee	Government Minister, 1932–1948, 1951–1954 and 1957–1965
13.	General Sean MacEoin	Minister for Justice and Defence

14.	Thomas D'Arcy McGee	Minister for Agriculture, and President of Council, Dominion of Canada
15.	Terence McManus	Brigadier General, United States Army
16.	Countess Constance Markievicz	First woman elected to the House of Commons
17.	Thomas F. Meagher	Governor of Montana
18.	John Mitchel	Prominent New York politician
19.	James Francis Xavier O'Brien	MP for Mayo, 1885–1895, and for Cork, 1895–1905
20.	Richard O'Gorman	Governor General of Newfoundland
21.	Ernie O'Malley	Irish representative at Chicago's World Fair of 1933, and a member of the Irish Academy of Letters
22.	John Boyle O'Reilly	Owner of the *Boston Pilot,* and writer of huge-selling novel, *Moondyne*
23.	A.M. Sullivan	MP for Louth, 1874–1880, and Cork, 1880–1881. Became father of A.M. Sullivan, the last Serjeant
24.	James Napper Tandy	Reprieved by Napoleon

School Reports (a) Delinquents
12 Irish people who did not finish their formal education

1. ERNEST BLYTHE
   Soldier, politican and writer, expelled from his Lisburn national school when he was only 11. His crime was insubordination.

2. MARK CAGNEY
   Former 2 FM disc jockey (now with Century), expelled from school, 'for being a little brat'.

3. MARY COUGHLAN
   Singer, expelled from school 'for mitching and hanging around with the lads'.

4. ROBERT EMMET
   United Irishman in the middle of a distinguished career at Trinity College, Dublin, when, at the age of 19, just prior to graduation, he voluntarily scratched his name from the college books, because the chancellor of the university, Lord Clare, had set up an inquisition into the students' political viewpoints.

5. GEORGE FARQUHAR
   Author of *The Beaux' Stratagem,* and *The Recruiting Officer.* Was a sizar at Trinity College Dublin when he was 17 but after 1½ years he left, probably after being expelled for a jest he made on a sacred exercise in the college.

6. EDWARD MacLYSAGHT
   Genealogist, left Oxford without taking a degree. Later in life, went to UCC and took a degree there.

7. WILLIAM O'BRIEN
   Nationalist politician and journalist, won a law scholarship to Queen's College, Cork. However, due to ill-health, he was unable to continue his studies, and from the age of 16 took up journalism, starting with Cork's *Daily Herald* in 1868.

8. SINEAD O'CONNOR
   Rock star, thrown out of Sion Hill convent for habitual 'bunking off'.

9. KEVIN O'HIGGINS
   Assassinated Cumann na nGaedhael politician, was expelled from Maynooth for drinking.

10. JOHN O'LEARY
    Fenian, President of the Supreme Council of the IRB from 1885–1907, destined to become a medical doctor, but did not complete his studies at Trinity College, Dublin.

11. PAIDI O'SHEA
    Kerry GAA football half-back, winner of 8 All-Ireland Senior Football Championship winners medals, was expelled from St Brendan's in Killarney for drinking.

12. CHARLES STEWART PARNELL
    Expelled from school in Kirk Langley, in Derbyshire. Earlier he had attended a school in Yeovil, Somerset, which was an all-girl establishment, but he was sent home having contracted typhoid there.

School Reports (b) Ahead of the Pack
The ages at which 24 famous Irish people left school

9	Sean O'Casey, playwright
	Paddy 'the Cope' Gallagher, co-operative founder
12	Patrick MacGill, writer
	Sean Kelly, cyclist
	Maureen Potter, actress
13	Douglas Hyde, President and Gaelgoir
	Finbarr Furey, singer
	Eamon Dunphy, soccer player and sports journalist
	Gillian Bowler, travel agent
$13\frac{1}{2}$	Lee Dunne, writer
14	Liam Brady, soccer player
	Brenda Fricker, actress
	John Cadden, RTE radio producer
	Peadar Kearney, composer of the national anthem
	Brendan Behan, playwright
	Seamus Murphy, sculptor
	Francis Ledwidge, poet
	Heno Magee, playwright
	John Morrow, novelist and writer
	Eileen Reid, singer
$14\frac{1}{2}$	Frank Paterson, tenor
	Barney McKenna, member of The Dubliners
15	Van Morrison, singer-songwriter
	Emmet Bergin, actor
	Gabriel Byrne, actor
	George Bernard Shaw, playwright
16	Larry Goodman, beef baron
$16\frac{1}{2}$	P.V. Doyle, hotelier

SAINTS AND SCHOLARS

Gift of the Gab
Famous Irish multi-linguists

1. RICHARD O'SULLIVAN BURKE (1838–1932)
   Dunmanway-born Fenian, learned several languages while travelling around the world as a seaman, during a 10-year period between 1850 and 1860.

2. DESMOND FITZGERALD (1889–1947)
   Sinn Fein, Cumann na nGaedhael and Fine Gael politician, and journalist, and father of former Taoiseach Garret FitzGerald. Was fluent in 6 languages, including Irish, which he learned in the county of his parents' birth, Kerry, he himself having been born in London.

3. WILLIAM ROWAN HAMILTON (1805–1865)
   Mathematician, also a renowned linguist. A child prodigy, he was familiar with the rudiments of 13 different languages at the age of 14. (They were Hebrew, Latin, Greek, French, Italian, Spanish, German, Syriac, Arabic, Sanskrit, Hindustani, Malay and Persian.) When he was only 7 years old, he was able to carry on a conversation in 9 languages.

4. REVEREND WILLIAM HENEBRY (1836–1916)
   Waterford-born Gaelic scholar, was an outstanding linguist, excelling in particular at Hebrew, Irish and English.

5. EDWARD HINCKS (1792–1866)
   Cork-born Assyriologist, was one of the most learned Egyptologists and Assyriologists of his age, so bright at languages that he was made a fellow at Trinity College, Dublin before he was 21.

6. AUGUSTUS HENRY KEANE (1833–1912)
Anthropologist, born in Cork, spent most of his long working life on registering and classifying almost every language known to man, and from all this data, he worked out a system of ethnology. Professor of Hindustani at University College London, 1882–1885.

7. ANNE LYTTON
Fluent in 8 different languages, and had a good knowledge of 8 more. Her fluent languages were French, German, Spanish, Italian, Portuguese, Latin, Greek and Hebrew. The others were Irish, Arabic, Russian, Syriac, Persian, Samarian, Ethiopic and Chaldee. Died at the age of 90.

8. ROBERT McADAM (1805–1895)
Belfast linguist, and brother of the geologist and librarian James McAdam. Fluent in 13 different languages. He had a particular gra for Irish, and encouraged its study.

9. JAMES CLARENCE MANGAN (1803–1849)
Poet, started studying European languages when, at the age of 15, he began working in a notary's office.

Survivors
Famous Irish people who lived to a ripe old age

120 St Kevin, founder of the Irish monastery at Glendalough, was reputed to be 120 years old when he died in AD 622.

112 Denis O'Hempsey, eighteenth-century Irish harpist, is believed to have lived through 3 different centuries. He is thought to have been born near Garvagh, Co Derry in about 1695. He lived 109 years of his life totally blind, losing his sight due to smallpox at the age of 3. He died in 1807.

111 The Hon. Katherine Plunkett, Ireland's oldest authenticated person ever, died on 14 October 1932 (39 days before her 112th birthday), having been born 111 years and 327 days previously, on 22 November 1820.

110 Catherine, the second wife of the 12th Earl of Desmond, who was born in Villierstown, Co Waterford, died at a great age, generally agreed to be 110.

107 Peggy Elliot, the 'Queen of Trasna Island' (which lies just off Devenish Island in Lough Erne), reputedly lived to the age of 107.

101 Greta Bowen, Dublin-born artist, exhibited to the first international exhibition of Naive art in London when she was in her 100th year in 1979. She died in her 102nd year in 1981.

100 Mary Harris Jones, Irish-born United States labour leader lived till she reached the century mark.
Charles Macklin, the eighteenth-century actor and dramatist, was reputedly 100 years old when he died in London in 1797.

99 Daniel Mannix, controversial Charleville, Co Cork-born Archbishop of Melbourne, died 4 months short of his 100th birthday, in Melbourne in 1963.

98 Edward MacLysaght, genealogist, was aged 98 years and 4 months when he died in Dublin in 1986.

Captain John Henry Webb, Kinsale-born sailor who served as Dublin's Harbour Master for 27 years, 1914–1941, was 98 when he died in 1968.

Martha Wilmot, the Cork-born adventurer and diarist, died in Dublin at the ripe old age of 98, in 1873.

97 Thomas Amory, writer and friend of Jonathan Swift, died in London aged at least 97.

Eileen Gray, interior designer and architect, was in her 98th year when she died in Paris in 1976.

Domhnall O'Buachalla, Governor-General of Ireland 1932–1937, died in 1963, aged 97.

George Noble Plunkett, antiquarian and politician, and father of the 1916 leader, Joseph Mary Plunkett, died in 1948, aged 97.

William Robinson, the Ballykilcavan, Co Laois-born gardening writer and authority, died at the age of 97.

96   Robert Childers Barton, signatory of the Anglo-Irish Treaty, was this age when he died at home in Annamoe, Co Wicklow in 1975.

Lucien Bull, Dublin-born inventor of the electrocardiograph in 1908, was 96 when he died in Paris in 1972.

Sinead de Valera, writer and wife of Eamon de Valera, died the day before her 65th wedding anniversary, at the age of 96.

Michael Fogarty, Bishop of Killaloe for almost 50 years (1904–1953), was made an archbishop at the age of 95, and died the following year.

Sir Richard Griffith, the geologist who compiled the Geological Map of Ireland, died in 1878 at the age of 96.

Norah Hoult, the writer best known for her classic book of short stories *Poor Women,* was 96 at the time of her death in 1984.

George Bernard Shaw, playwright, died at the age of 96, having been made a Freeman of Dublin at the age of 90. He wrote up until his death.

Mary Swanzy, painter, died in 1978 at the age of 96.

95   Joseph Deakin, Irish-born Olympic gold medal winner in 1908 (in the 3-man 3-mile team event) who ran in the Surrey Athletic Club's Handicap race up until his 90th year, died in 1972 at the age of 95.

94   Sir Richard John Griffith, Dublin-born geologist and civil engineer, died just 2 days after his 94th birthday in his Dublin house on Fitzwilliam Square.

Billy Lord, Shamrock Rovers guru for many years, was 94 when he died in 1985.

Professor Arthur Luce, Trinity College, Dublin philosophy academic, and a Fellow of the university for a record 65 years, died at the age of 94.

Sean MacEntee, revolutionary, and long-serving Fianna Fail government minister, died in Dublin at the beginning of 1984, aged 94.

93 Kathleen Clarke, Limerick-born republican, a TD and senator, and wife of 1916 leader Tom Clarke, died at 93.

Mary Dwyer, the widow of United Irishman Michael Dwyer, lived 46 years after her husband's death, dying in Sydney in 1861.

Richard Ashe King, Co Clare-born writer of such popular novels as *The Wearing of the Green* (1886), died in 1932, aged 93.

Peadar O'Donnell, socialist and writer, died at the age of 93 in Dublin in 1986.

The Reverend Matthew 'The General' Ryan, land agitator, died in 1937 at this age.

Grizell Steevens, twin-sister of the founder of Dr Steevens' Hospital in Dublin, who outlived her brother by 36 years, and ensured the success of the hospital, died aged 93.

92 Chester Beatty, founder of the Chester Beatty Library in Shrewsbury Road in Dublin, and an Honorary Citizen of Ireland, died in Monte Carlo in 1968, at 92.

Eamon de Valera, the former Taoiseach and President of Ireland, died 8 months after his wife, when he was 92, in 1975, having held the office of President past his 90th birthday.

Frank Duff, founder of the Legion of Mary in 1921, died in the Morning Star hostel (which he founded for down-and-outs) at the age of 91 in 1980.

Paddy 'The Cope' Gallagher, who established a co-operative in Co Donegal, died in that county in 1966, aged 92.

Sir Hugh Gough, Waterford-born general who defied instructions regarding the imposition of Home Rule in Northern Ireland, died in London in 1963.

Arthur Power, painter and author of *Conversations with James Joyce,* died at this age in 1984.

Sir Hans Sloane, Co Down-born naturalist and physician, whose collection of specimens made up the main bulk of the British Museum, died 3 months short of his 93rd birthday.

91 William James Brennan-Whitmore, last surviving commandant of the 1916 Rising, died in December 1977, aged 91.

The O'Gorman Mahon, Charles J. P. Mahon, nineteenth-century soldier and politician, died in London at the age of 91 in 1981, despite reputedly taking part in at least 13 duels.

Edith Somerville, novelist partner of Violet Martin (Martin Ross), died in 1949, living 34 years after Violet's death.

90 Padraic Colum, Longford-born poet and dramatist, was just over a month past his 90th birthday when he died in 1972 in Enfield, Connecticut in the United States.

Tom Johnson, trade unionist and Labour Party leader, died in 1963 in Dublin, aged 90.

Patrick McGilligan, government minister, Attorney General and lawyer, reached his 90th birthday.

John McHale, Archbishop of Tuam from 1934 till his death, died (actively preaching at Mass) in Tuam in 1881, at the age of 90.

Margaret Pearse, sister of Patrick Pearse, a senator for 30 years from 1933 until she died aged 90 in 1968; she was given a State funeral.

Rebecca West, the Co Kerry-born British journalist and novelist, worked right up until her death at 90.

The Age of Aquarius

Well-known Irish people who share the same date of birth with another personality of repute

January

4-1-1930   Tras Honan, Seanad Ceann Comhairle and Iain Cuthbertson, Scottish TV and theatre actor

6-1-1942   Noel Pearson, theatre impresario and Terry Venables, English footballer, manager

8-1-1941   Noel Gilmore, ex-head of Bord Bainne and Graham Chapman, *Monty Python* actor

9-1-1929   Brian Friel, playwright and Brian Farrell, political interviewer

10-1-1910   'Lugs' Brannigan, Dublin Garda and Sir Cecil Bateman, banker

16-1-1941   Michael Nesbitt, Arnott's boss and Christine Truman, tennis star

17-1-1860   Douglas Hyde, Irish President and Gaelic scholar, and Anton Chekov, French writer

25-1-1949   Tom Paulin, poet and Phil Boyer, English soccer player

31-1-1944   John Boland, former Fine Gael government minister and Jessica Walter, United States film actress

February

2-2-1882   James Joyce, writer and James Stephens, writer

6-2-1922   Bishop Michael Harty and Patrick McNee, British actor (Steed in *The Avengers*)

6-2-1933	Michael Viney, writer and journalist and Leslie Crowther, TV presenter (*The Price Is Right*)
12-2-1923	James Chichester-Clark, Northern Ireland Prime Minister and Franco Zeffirelli, Italian film director
14-2-1951	Alan Shatter, Fine Gael politician and Kevin Keegan, soccer player
22-2-1900	Sean O'Faolain, writer and Luis Bunuel, film director
24-2-1948	Dermot Earley, Roscommon GAA football great and Denis 'Minder' Waterman, actor
26-2-1928	Michael Killeen, IDA boss and Fats Domino, musician
28-2-1940	Jim Sherwin, RTE presenter and Mario Andretti, world champion car driver

March

2-3-1931	Paddy Cooney, former Fine Gael government minister and Mikhail Gorbachev, Soviet leader
2-3-1949	Rory Gallagher, rock guitarist and J. P. R. Williams, Welsh rugby full-back
9-3-1934	Joe Foyle, writer and Yuri Gagarin, Russian cosmonaut
19-3-1916	Lady Dillon of Wicklow and Irving Wallace, United States writer
20-3-1939	Kevin Flynn, rugby international and Brian Mulroney, Canadian Prime Minister
24-3-1909	Jefferson Smurfit, founder of Smurfit Group and Tommy Trinder, British comedian
25-3-1921	Bishop McCormack and Simone Signoret, film actress
26-3-1856	Sir John Lavery, painter and William Massey Ferguson, Irish-born Prime Minister of New Zealand

| 27-3-1917 | Harry West, Unionist politician and Cyrus Vance, United States Secretary of State |
| 29-3-1935 | Bishop James Mahaffey and Norman Tebbit, British politician |

April

9-4-1926	Gerry Fitt, SDLP politician and Hugh Hefner, Playboy founder
10-4-1938	Tim Phillips, Ballyfree businessman and Glen Campbell, country singer
13-4-1917	Olivia Robertson, novelist and Howard Keel, actor and singer
13-4-1952	Jonjo O'Neill, jockey and Peter Davidson, *Dr Who* actor no. 5
17-4-1946	Henry Kelly, TV personality and Clare Francis, yachtswoman and writer
19-4-1936	Seamus Pattison, Labour TD and Dudley Moore, actor
25-4-1941	Peter Sutherland, EC Commissioner and Bjorn Ulvaeus, Abba singer
26-4-1927	Philomena Garvey, golfer and Jack Douglas, British comic actor
26-4-1962	Jacko McDonagh, soccer player and Josimar, Brazilian soccer player
27-4-1927	Philip Flynn, Abbey actor and Coretta Scott-King, singer and wife of Martin Luther King

May

| 4-5-1928 | Thomas Kinsella, poet and Mohammed Hosni Mubarak, Egyptian leader |
| 8-5-1942 | Terry Neill, soccer player and manager and Benoit Dauga, French rugby player |

8-5-1944	Paddy O'Hanlon, former SDLP politician and Gary Glitter, singer
9-5-1946	Homan Potterton, ex-gallery director and Candice Bergin, actress
12-5-1941	Muiris MacCongail, academic and Ian Drury, singer
15-5-1935	Barry Desmond, Labour Party politician and Dennis Potter, playwright
22-5-1943	Mairead Corrigan, Peace People leader and Michael Noonan, former Fine Gael government minister
23-5-1951	Henry Mountcharles, owner of Slane Castle and Anatoly Karpov, former world chess champion
24-5-1928	William Trevor, writer and Stanley Baxter, British comedian

June

1-6-1937	Tommy Wade, showjumper and Rosaleen Linehan, actress/comedian
6-6-1932	Julia O'Faolain, journalist and writer and Billie Whitelaw, British actress
6-6-1951	Frank Fahy, Junior Minister and Russell Grant, astrologer
10-6-1926	Kevin McNamara, ex-Archbishop of Dublin and June Havers, Hollywood actress
18-6-1901	Denis Johnston, writer and Jeannette McDonald, Hollywood singer/actress
19-6-1940	Sister Stanislaus Kennedy, charity organiser and Paul 'Ted Bovis' Shane from TV's *Hi Di Hi!!*
25-6-1942	Padraic White, IDA boss and Eddie Large, British TV comedian
28-6-1926	Paddy Belton, ex-Dublin TD and Mel Brooks, film director

July

1-7-1934   James Liddy, poet and Jean Marsh, actress, Rose in *Upstairs, Downstairs*

4-7-1928   Stephen Boyd, Belfast-born film actor and Gina Lollabrigida, Italian screen actress

5-7-1938   Brendan Halligan, Labour politician and Bord na Mona boss and Alan Kelly, Irish soccer goal-keeper

6-7-1926   Proinsias MacAnna, academic and Janet Leigh, *Psycho* actress

6-7-1936   Bobby Molloy, Progressive Democrats politician and Dave Allen, Irish comedian in Britain

10-7-1956   Frank Stapleton, Irish soccer player and Tommy Carmody, Irish jump jockey

14-7-1918   Lewis Rhattigan, man of theatre, and Ingmar Bergman, Swedish film director

21-7-1928   John B. Keane, Kerry playwright and Isaac Stern, violinist

21-7-1935   Tony Doyle, actor (played the priest in *The Riordans*) and Julian Pettifer, British TV presenter

August

3-8-1924   Jim Gibbons, former Fianna Fail government minister and Leon Uris, novelist

3-8-1958   Feargal Sharkey, pop star and David Feherty, professional golfer

6-8-1927   Richard Murphy, poet and Andy Warhol, artist

8-8-1944   Sean Barrett, former Fine Gael government minister and George Armstrong, soccer forward

10-8-1926   Peter Barry, former Fine Gael government minister and Eddie Fisher, actor

22-8-1908	Mervyn Wall, Dublin writer and Henri Cartier-Bresson, photographer
31-8-1913	Jack Doyle, boxer and entertainer and Sir Bernard Lovell, British astronomer
31-8-1945	Van Morrison, rock star and Itzhak Perlman, famous Israeli violinist

September

4-9-1935	Pauline Bewick, artist and Michael Noonan, Minister for Defence
6-9-1954	Johnny Fingers, ex-Boomtown Rat and Stephanie Zimbalist, *Remington Steele* actress
8-9-1923	John Cowley, *Riordans* actor and Alan Weeks, BBC sports commentator
10-9-1939	Mark Killilea, Fianna Fail TD, David Hamilton, British DJ and Cynthia Lennon, ex-wife of Beatle John Lennon
16-9-1925	Charles J. Haughey, Taoiseach, B.B. King, famed United States guitarist and Charlie Bird, also United States guitarist
24-9-1936	Bishop John Magee, ex-Vatican official and Jim Henson, founder of The Muppets
27-9-1948	Joe Dowling, theatre producer/director/actor, Olivia Newton-John, singer and Michele Dotrice actress (Betty in *Some Mothers Do Have 'Em*)
29-9-1946	Michael Keating, ex-Progressive Democrats and deputy leader and Patricia Hodge, British actress (Jemima Shore)

October

1-10-1921	Philip Greene, soccer commentator and Walter Mathau, United States film actor
2-10-1945	Terry Leyden, Fianna Fail and Don McLean, singer/songwriter

5-10-1941 Frank Patterson, tenor and Deirdre Friel, RTE producer

6-10-1939 Maria Simmons-Gooding, painter and Melvyn Bragg, writer and TV presenter

12-10-1920 Christy Ring, illustrious Cork hurler and Lord Soames, British politician

18-10-1928 George Colley, ex Fianna Fail Tanaiste and Melina Mercouri, Greek actress and government minister

20-10-1941 Mike Murphy, RTE TV and radio personality and the late Stewart Parker, playwright

24-10-1948 Tom Grace, rugby wing-threequarter, Phil Bennett, Welsh rugby out-half, and Paul and Barry Ryan, twin United States singers

25-10-1955 Ritchie Connor, Offaly footballer and Glynis Barber, *Dempsey and Makepeace* actress

28-10-1948 Denis Taylor, snooker player and Mike Channon, English soccer forward

November

3-11-1935 Albert Reynolds, Minister for Finance and Jeremy Brett, British actor

8-11-1961 Sean Haughey, Fianna Fail present mayor of Dublin, and Leif Garrett, pop singer

14-11-1935 Augustine Martin, writer and academic and King Hussein of Jordan

22-11-1932 Martin Dully, Bord Failte boss and Robert Vaughan, *Man from U.N.C.L.E.* actor

24-11-1952 Eamonn Coghlan, middle distance athlete and Andrea Lynch, British sprint athlete

29-11-1910 Cyril Cusack, actor and Martin O'Direain, poet in Irish

27-11-1921 Sean MacReamoinn, broadcaster and Alexander Dubcek, Czech leader of the 1960s

28-11-1931 Dearbhla Murphy, writer and Hope Lange, U.S. movie actress

December

1-12-1928 Denis O'Donoghue, academic and Keith Michell, actor

1-12-1945 Gilbert O'Sullivan, singer/songwriter and Bette Midler, actress and singer

14-12-1950 Philip Orr, rugby international prop forward and Vickie Michele, actress in *Allo! Allo!* (formerly 'Sally O'Brien')

16-12-1939 Barney McKenna, member of The Dubliners group and actress Liv Ullman

24-12-1915 Thomas Murphy, ex-UCD President and William Randolph Hearst, publisher

25-12-1924 Jim Tunney, former Fianna Fail government minister and Rod Serling, presenter of TV's *The Twilight Zone*

30-12-1951 Gay Mitchell, Fine Gael TD and Clive Ferguson, Lurgan-born TV reporter

Promise cut short
Irish people who did not live to fulfil their promise or ability

All of these people listed below did not get past the age of 40, that age often recognised as the age of maturity.

Died age

40 SEAN O'RIADA
Musician and composer, only 2 months passed the age of 40 when he died in London in October 1971.
ADRIAN STOKES
Pathologist, was working on a cure for Yellow Fever, when he himself contracted the disease and died 4 days later in 1927.

39 ELIZABETH CASEY
Author of the pioneering work *Illustrious Irishwomen* in 1877, burnt to death by accident in Fairview in 1894.
THOMAS PARNELL
Poet and archdeacon, friend of Jonathan Swift, died at the age of 39 in Chester in 1679.

38 OLIVER BOND
United Irishman, died without warning in prison while waiting to be hanged in September 1798.
LAETITIA PILKINGTON
Friendship with Jonathan Swift is detailed in her *Memoirs,* was 38 when she died in 1750.
JOHN MILLINGTON SYNGE
Playwright, work includes *The Playboy of the Western World, Riders to the Sea,* and *Deirdre of the Sorrows,* died of a lymphatic tumour at the age of 38.

37 MARY-ANNE COSGRAVE
Trim, Co Meath-born nun, known in Africa by the name Mother Patrick, founded and staffed hospitals in Salisbury, Bulawayo and Gwelo, died at 37.

GERALD GRIFFIN
Dramatist, poet and novelist, best known for his novel, *The Collegians,* died at 37 in 1840.

ALEXANDER MacDONNELL
Belfast-born chess master, hailed as one of the finest grand masters of his day, died in London in 1835, before a rematch could be played against his great French adversary, Louis de Labourdonnais.

CHARLES A. READ
Author of the 4-volume *Cabinet of Irish Literature,* died in Surrey aged 37.

36 ETHNA CARBERY
Poet, wife of fellow-writer, Seamus MacManus, died shortly after their wedding in 1866.

EOGHAN RUA O'SUILLEABHAIN
Eighteenth-century Kerry poet, died from a fever in 1784, only a few days after being hurt in a drunken brawl in Killarney.

EDEL QUINN
Legion of Mary envoy in Africa, died 12 years after being diagnosed of tuberculosis, in Nairobi.

35 JOHN ST JOHN LONG
Newcastle West-born painter and quack doctor, died in London at the age of 35 in 1834.

MARY LETITIA HOWARD
'Princess of Connemara', best known for the huge-selling novel *Julia Howard,* died in childbirth in 1850, in New York.

JOHN MAGEE THE YOUNGER
Proprietor of the *Dublin Evening Post,* died in prison while serving 2 years for libel in 1814.

SIR EDWARD LOVETT PEARCE
Meath-born architect, designed the Houses of Parliament in College Green, Dublin (now the Bank of Ireland), died from an abscess in 1733.

33 RUAIDHRI O'DONNELL, THE FIRST EARL OF TIR CHONAILL
Died young in Rome in 1608.

FATHER EUGENE O'GROWNEY
Leader of the movement for the revival of the Irish language in the late nineteenth century, died in Los Angeles aged only 33, in 1899.

FANNY PARNELL
Poet famous for *Hold the Harvest*. A younger sister of Charles Stewart Parnell, she died at this age in 1892.

32 THOMAS ASHE
Republican/revolutionary, died from being forcibly fed after only 5 days of a hunger strike in 1917.

CHARLES WOLFE
Dublin-born Ulster poet. His poems *The Burial of Sir John Moore after Corunna* has been memorised by generations of schoolchildren in England. Died of consumption in 1823, aged only 32.

31 JOHN HENDERSON
Eccentric Limerick-born connoisseur of eighteenth-century low-life; slept in daytime, was active at night. Smoked opium and drank alcohol to excess. Died in Oxford in 1788.

RED HUGH O'DONNELL
Hero of the Battle of the Yellow Ford in 1598, fell ill suddenly in Spain in 1602, and died in Simancas in 1602.

30 THOMAS DAVIS
Poet and founder of *The Nation,* died from a fever shortly before his 31st birthday, in 1845.

PATRICK HENEY
Musician, composed the music (to the words of Peadar Kearney) of the Irish national anthem, died at age 30.

29 GEORGE FARQUHAR
Dramatist, best-known works are *The Recruiting Officer* and *The Beaux' Stratagem,* died in abject poverty at 29.

28 PATRICK MURPHY
Co Down-born giant, reached a height of 8 feet, 1 inch. Died while touring in Marseilles, aged 28.

WILLIAM ROONEY
Journalist, toured Ireland in an effort to help revive the Irish language, died in 1901, aged 28.

27 THOMAS DERMODY
Poet, bon viveur, died in poverty, from the excesses of alcohol in 1802, at 27.
MARIA GUNNING, COUNTESS OF COVENTRY
One of 2 celebrated beauties, daughters of a poor Roscommon man, who married into English nobility. However, excessive use of white lead paint as a cosmetic caused her to die aged only 27, having borne 5 children.
CHRISTOPHER EMMET
An older brother (by 17 years) of the patriot, Robert Emmet, died in 1788, at the age of 27. He had written a noted allegorical poem about the downfall of the British Empire. Robert, who was only 10 years old when his brother died, was hugely affected by it (in fact he himself was to die at an earlier age still).

26 MARIA CAMPION
Irish actress, died at 26.
SARAH CURRAN
Sweetheart of Robert Emmet, died at 26, 5 years after Emmet.

23 JOHN KEEGAN CASEY
Poet and author of the ballad *The Rising of the Moon,* had not reached his 24th birthday when he died of tuberculosis in March 1870.
LIAM WHELAN
Soccer player, capped 4 times for Ireland was 23 years old when he became the only Irishman to die in the infamous Manchester United airplane crash in Munich airport, on 6 February 1958.

18 JEREMIAH DANIEL MURPHY
Eighteenth-century language expert. His ability to pick up different languages astounded his contemporaries (he had mastered Greek, Latin, French, Portuguese, Spanish, German and Irish), died at 18 of a heart disease.

CAPITAL SHIFTS

Deep in Canadian Woods
Irish placenames abroad

Listed below, in alphabetical order, are places outside Ireland which bear the same name as place names in Ireland. Many of these places have been called after the Irish original, and some of those whose origins are otherwise are explained. Places in Ireland which have a name which can be termed as not indigenous (like Westport, which has had a whole book listing the places abroad with the same name), are generally avoided or given less attention. Places like Martinique (aka 'The Other Emerald Isle'), have many hamlets, districts, beaches, pubs etc. which reflect its Irish connections.

1. ANTRIM
   ANTRIM COUNTY, in the north-west of Michigan in the United States, touching Grand Traverse Bay on Lake Michigan, is about half the size of Ireland's Antrim, has a population of 16,000, and has as its county seat, the town of Bellaire.

2. ARMAGH
   ARMAGH is a village in south Quebec, Canada, with a population of almost 1,000. There is also a borough in Indiana County in Pennsylvania called Armagh.

3. AUBURN
   There are many towns in the United States called after 'sweet Auburn', as idolised by Goldsmith in *The Deserted Village*. Among them are:
   (a) AUBURN, Alabama; population in 1980 of 28,471, the home of Auburn University, which was founded in 1865. The city is situated about 50 miles east of the state capital, Montgomery.

(b)   AUBURN, Maine; in south-western Maine, on the Androscoggin river opposite Lewiston, 32 miles north-east of Portland; population of 23,000; a major shoe manufacturing city.

(c)   AUBURN, Washington; a satellite town of Seattle and Tacoma, population of 26,417.

(d)   AUBURN, Massachusetts; small city just off Interstate 90, south of Worcester, Mass; population of over 14,000.

(e)   AUBURN, New York; population in 1980 of 32,548; situated in the heart of the Finger Lakes district, 25 miles south-west of Syracuse, on the outlet of Owasco Lake.

4. BRANDON
BRANDON, Manitoba, Canada; lying west of Winnipeg, on the Assiniboine River; important commercial centre of the wheat area. It has a population of over 30,000, and has oil refining and agricultural equipment industries.

5. BALLINA
BALLINA, New South Wales, 376 miles north of Sydney; port on the mouth of the Richmond River, with a population of over 6,000 people. It is thought that its name did not in fact come from the Mayo town, but from an aboriginal phrase meaning 'place where oysters are plentiful'.

6. BELFAST
(a)   BELFAST, Waldo County, Maine, United States; port named after Belfast by Samuel Miller, who emigrated to America in 1770. Population of about 6,000, mainly reliant on tourism.

(b)   BELFAST, New Zealand; a northern satellite of the capital Christchurch, situated on the North Road, about 5 miles from the city centre.

(c)   BELFAST, Canada; small coastal town on Hillsborough Bay, facing the capital of the Prince Edward Island province of Canada, Charlottetown, from which it is about 30 miles by road.

7. CARLOW

CARLOW ISLAND; small town in eastern Maine, a few miles from the Canadian border.

8. CLARE

CLARE has four places abroad named after it:

(a) the beautiful small town of Clare in Suffolk, England, situated on the River Stour.

(b) a town in South Australia, which was called after the county from where the first settler hailed. It has a population of 2,100, is in the middle of a wine-growing area, and is also a reserve for Springyback Eucalyptus trees.

(c) a town in Webster County, Iowa, in the United States (10 miles north of Fort Dodge).

(d) Clare County, in central Michigan in the United States; population of 23,000.

9. CLIFDEN

CLIFDEN, New Zealand; small town near the south coast of South Island, on the Waiao River, about 12 miles north of Te Waewae Bay, 40 miles north-west of Invercargill.

10. CLONMEL

CLONMEL is a town on the island of Jamaica.

11. COLERAINE

(a) COLERAINE, Minnesota; small town in Atasca County about 10 miles north-west of the city of Grand Rapids; population of about 1,000.

(b) COLERAINE, Australia; just west of the town of Hamilton in Victoria, about 150 miles west of Melbourne.

(c) COLERAINE, Quebec Province, Canada, about 60 miles south of Quebec.

12. CONNAUGHT

CONNAUGHT, Ontario; small Canadian town about 10 miles from the Northern Route of the Trans Canadian Highway, in the vast lake-covered interior of Ontario province.

13. DERRY
    (a) DERRY, Rockingham County, United States; in
         south-east New Hampshire; population of 13,000,
         called after Derry in 1827. It is noted for horse racing
         on ice in winter, and as a place where the poet
         Robert Frost once taught.
    (b) DERRY, Pennsylvania, United States; satellite town
         for the city of Pittsburgh, about 30 miles east of it;
         population of 3,000.
    (c) DERRY, New Mexico, United States; small town on
         the Rio Grande about 100 miles north-east of El
         Paso.

14. DONEGAL
    DONEGAL is a small borough in Westmoreland County, in
    south-west Pennsylvania in the United States, about 30
    miles south-west of Pittsburgh, with a population of little
    more than 250.

15. DUBLIN
    (a) DUBLIN, California, United States; unincorporated
         city in the San Francisco Bay Area, near Oakland,
         with a population of about 13,000, known for its
         shopping facilities.
    (b) DUBLIN, Georgia, United States; population of
         16,000; the largest 'Dublin' outside Ireland. Situated
         on the Oconee River, about halfway between Atlanta
         and Savannah. It was named in honour of the Irish
         wife of a Scots-Irish founder of the town, Jonathan
         Sawyer, in 1812.
    (c) DUBLIN, New Hampshire, United States; highest
         village in New England, situated on Monadnock
         Mountain, about 1,493 feet above sea level. It is
         about 80 miles from Boston.
    (d) DUBLIN, Ontario, Canada; small village in the
         isthmus in the Great Lakes area, 20 miles east of
         Lake Huron, 50 miles north of Lake Erie, and 100
         miles west of Toronto, on Lake Ontario.
    (e) DUBLIN, South Australia; small petrol-stop village
         about 20 miles north of Adelaide, near the gulf of St
         Vincent.

(f) DUBLIN, Texas, United States; situated about halfway between Abilene and Waco; gets its name, not from our capital city, but from the phrase 'Double Inn', because it once boasted 2 bars. However it does bear all the hallmarks of being Irish, having a Grafton Street, a Patrick Street, a Camden Street, and an O'Neill Street. It is in Erath County, and is the birthplace of the famous golfer, Ben Hogan. Its population is about 2,700.

(g) DUBLIN. There are also many other Dublins in the United States. Among them are those of Alaska, Maryland (population c. 500), Florida, Indiana (population c. 1,000), Iowa, Virginia, Arkansas, Ohio (population c. 600), North Carolina (a town of about 500 population, with a local rule barring alcohol and dancing), Kentucky and 2 in Pennsylvania.

16. DUNDALK
(a) DUNDALK, Maryland, United States; sub-division of Baltimore County, on the outskirts of Baltimore. With a population of more than 70,000, it is in a strongly industrialised area, and contains one of the largest steel manufacturing plants in the world.

(b) DUNDALK, Canada; small town in Ontario, 50 miles north-west of Toronto.

17. ENNIS
(a) ENNIS, Texas, United States; 30 miles south of Dallas, just off Interstate 45, population of 12,110 in 1980.

(b) ENNIS, Montana, United States; small town in Madison County, on the Madison River, near a Lake Ennis, about halfway between the city of Butte and Yellowstone National Park.

18. GALWAY
GALWAY; village in the dairy farming area of Saratoga County in eastern New York State, United States.

19. KENMARE
KENMARE, North Dakota; small town on Highway 55 in north-west corner of the state, in Ward County, on the Des Lacs River. Its population is just over 1,500.

20. KERRY
   KERRY; village in the Welsh mountains, near the river Severn, just south-east of the town of Newtown in Powys.

21. KILDARE
   (a) KILDARE; town in Kay County in north Oklahoma, near the state boundary with Kansas.
   (b) KILDARE, Texas; small town very near the state's boundaries with Louisiana and Arkansas, lying half-way between Texarkana and Shreveport. There is also a Cape Kildare on Prince Edward Island in Canada.

22. KILKENNY
   KILKENNY, Minnesota, United States; village in La Sueur County, about 40 miles south-west of Minneapolis/St Paul.

23. KILLALA
   KILLALA LAKE; small lake about 20 miles from the northern coastline of the world's biggest freshwater lake, Lake Superior, in the province of Ontario.

24. KILLALOE
   KILLALOE; small town in Ontario, about 90 miles due west of Ottawa.

25. KINSALE
   KINSALE, Maryland, small town about 10 miles from the birthplace of George Washington in Virginia, near where the Potomac River flows into Chesapeake Bay.

26. LIMERICK
   LIMERICK, Maine, United States; small town, founded in 1777, about 25 miles east of the state's largest city, Portland, and is only 10 miles from the state boundary with new Hampshire. It gets its name from the birthplace of the father of one of its founders, James O'Sullivan. It has a population of only 1,300, and is situated in a dairy farming area.

27. LISTOWEL
   LISTOWEL, Ontario, Canada; town 60 miles east of Toronto in Canada. Nearby are smaller towns with names like Dublin, Dundalk, Waterford, etc.

28. LONGFORD
    (a) LONGFORD, Tasmania; small town of 1,700 population in north central Tasmania; named after an early settler's home county. It is a sheep rearing area, and has a world-renowned road racing circuit nearby.
    (b) LONGFORD, New Zealand; small village in the inland mountain area of Nelson province of South Island, 40 miles east of the big town of Westport.

29. MAYO
    MAYO, Florida, United States; the county seat of Lafayette County in north Florida, near the Suwannee River, on Interstate U.S. 27. The county's population is just over 4,000 people, with Mayo having about 800 residents.

30. NEWRY
    NEWRY has 3 places of the same name: a small town in Oxford County, Maine, a small town near Altoona, west of Pittsburgh Pennsylvania, and a small town in the northwestern part of Northern Territory, Australia.

31. ROSCOMMON
    ROSCOMMON COUNTY, Michigan, United States; about half the size of Ireland's county, and has as its county seat, Roscommon. Situated in north-central Michigan, the county has 16,000 residents, the town itself having less than 1,000.

32. SLIGO
    SLIGO is a small borough in Clarion County in west central Pennsylvania, having only about 800 residents. It is about 50 miles north-east of the city of Pittsburgh.

33. ULSTER
    ULSTER COUNTY, New York State, United States; about the size of County Kerry; population of about 150,000. Containing the Catskill Mountains, it is one of the most beautiful parts of New York State, and as it is only about 75 miles north of New York City, it is a favourite retreat for affluent, weekending New Yorkers.

34. WATERFORD
    (a) WATERFORD, Connecticut, United States; a rural community with a population of about 18,000, contains the home of the Eugene O'Neill Memorial Theatre Foundation, situated on the River Thames.
    (b) WATERFORD, Maine, United States; in Oxford County; birthplace of the popular nineteenth-century humorist Artemus Ward.
    (c) WATERFORD, Michigan, United States; unincorporated town in Oakland County, just outside Detroit, with a population of 64,250 in 1980. This gives it a population of over 20,000 more than the Irish city whose name it bears.

35. WESTPORT
    WESTPORT, New Zealand; the site of one of the country's principal sources of bituminous coal. Gold was discovered here in 1859. The town's population is over 5,000.

36. WEXFORD
    WEXFORD COUNTY, Michigan, United States; population of over 25,000; contains the town of Cadillac, which gave its name to the popular car, and is about the same size as Ireland's Co Wexford.

The American Connection
92 United States County names bearing Irish surnames

Below are listed 92 Irish surnames which give their names to a total of 155 United States counties (averaging 3 per American state)

County Name	State
1. Aiken:	South Carolina
2. Allen:	Indiana, Kansas, Louisiana, Ohio
3. Anderson:	Kansas

4.	Ashe:	North Carolina
5.	Bailey:	Texas
6.	Barry:	Michigan, Missouri
7.	Barton:	Kansas, Missouri
8.	Bennett:	South Dakota
9.	Bowman:	North Dakota
10.	Bradley:	Arkansas, Tennessee
11.	Briscoe:	Texas
12.	Burke:	Georgia, North Carolina, North Dakota
13.	Butler:	Alabama, Iowa, Missouri, Pennsylvania
14.	Carroll:	Illinois, Indiana, Iowa, Kentucky, Maryland, Mississippi, New Hampshire, Ohio, Tennessee, Virginia
15.	Casey:	Kentucky
16.	Clark:	Illinois, Indiana, Kentucky, Wisconsin
17.	Clarke:	Alabama, Georgia, Iowa, Virginia
18.	Clinton:	Indiana, Kentucky, Michigan
19.	Colbert:	Alabama
20.	Cooke:	Texas
21.	Crowley:	Colorado
22.	Dawson:	Montana, Nebraska
23.	Dillon:	South Carolina
24.	Dwyer:	Tennessee
25.	Early:	Georgia
26.	Ellis:	Oklahoma
27.	Emmet:	Iowa
28.	Fallon:	Montana
29.	Fannin:	Georgia

30.	Fergus:	Montana
31.	Fleming:	Kentucky
32.	Garrett:	Maryland
33.	Garvin:	Oklahoma
34.	Gibson:	Indiana, Tennessee
35.	Gilchrist:	Florida
36.	Giles:	Tennessee, Virginia
37.	Gillespie:	Texas
38.	Grady:	Oklahoma
39.	Gregg:	Texas
40.	Greene:	Alabama, Arkansas, Illinois, Mississippi, Pennsylvania, Tennessee
41.	Hale:	Alabama
42.	Harney:	Oregon (the largest in the state, bigger than the Irish province of Munster)
43.	Harris:	Texas (has a population of $2\frac{1}{2}$ million, containing as it does the city of Houston)
44.	Harrison:	Indiana, Iowa, Kentucky
45.	Hayes:	Nebraska
46.	Holmes:	Mississippi, Ohio
47.	Hughes:	Oklahoma, South Dakota
48.	Hyde:	South Dakota
49.	Jennings:	Indiana
50.	Kane:	Illinois, Utah
51.	Kearney:	Kansas, Nebraska
52.	Kerr:	Texas
53.	Lee:	Alabama, Arkansas
54.	Lynn:	Texas

55.	Lyon:	Iowa, Minnesota
56.	McCormick:	South Carolina
57.	McCracken:	Kentucky
58.	McCreary:	Kentucky
59.	McCurtain:	Oklahoma
60.	McDonough:	Illinois
61.	McLennan:	Texas (containing the city of Waco, the county has a population of 170,000)
62.	Mathews:	Virginia
63.	Meade:	Kansas, Kentucky, South Dakota
64.	Meagher:	Montana
65.	Mitchell:	Iowa
66.	Moore:	North Carolina, Texas
67.	Morrow:	Oregon
68.	Morton:	Kansas
69.	Murray:	Minnesota, Oklahoma, Georgia
70.	Nash:	North Carolina
71.	Nolan:	Texas
72.	O'Brien:	Iowa
73.	Owen:	Indiana, Kentucky
74.	Pierce:	North Dakota, Wisconsin, Georgia
75.	Power:	Idaho
76.	Preston:	West Virginia
77.	Rice:	Minnesota
78.	Rogers:	Oklahoma
79.	Russell:	Alabama
80.	Sharkey:	Mississippi

81.	Sheridan:	Montana, Nebraska, North Dakota, Wyoming
82.	Stanley:	South Dakota
83.	Stephens:	Oklahoma, Georgia
84.	Stevens:	Kansas, Washington
85.	Sullivan:	New Hampshire, New York, Pennsylvania
86.	Talbot:	Maryland, Georgia
87.	Toole:	Montana
88.	Tyrrell:	North Carolina
89.	Walsh:	North Dakota
90.	Walton:	Georgia
91.	Ward:	North Dakota
92.	Weld:	Colorado

Trail of Glory

25 Irishmen with places thoughout the world named after them

1. JOHN BALL
   Dublin-born, first President of the Alpine Club, who wrote the well-known *Alpine Guide,* is remembered by an Alpine pass, Passa di Ball, and by an Alpine summit, Cima di Ball.

2. GEORGE BERKELEY (1685–1753)
   Philosopher, has many places abroad named in his honour. The city of Berkeley, California, and its famous university are both dedicated to him.

3. JAMES BRYCE (1838–1922)
Belfast-born Liberal politician, Chief Secretary in Ireland 1905–1907. Was also a keen mountaineer and has a mountain in the Rockies of North America named in his honour.

4. EDMUND BURKE (1729–1797)
Statesman and writer, has a county in the American state of Georgia named after him.

5. ROBERT O'HARA BURKE
St Clerans, Co Galway-born explorer, among the first to cross the Australian continent from south to north. Burketown, near the coast of the Gulf of Carpentaria in Australia, is named after him. It is very near the spot where, in 1861, he and his companion Willis, reached the tidal waters of the Flinders River, which feeds the Gulf.

6. THE 2nd EARL OF CALEDON
Governor of the Cape of Good Hope 1801–1811, gives his name to 2 geographical features in South Africa: the Caledon River, on which stands Maseru, the capital of Lesotho, and to a satellite town of Capetown, Caledon, 50 miles to the city's south-west.

7. SAINT GALL
Hermit who built a 'cell' dwelling on a site in north-east modern-day Switzerland in AD 614, has a canton there named after him. St Gall Canton, bordering Lake Constance, has an area of 2,012 square kilometres, and its population is about 400,000. The canton capital, of the same name, was established around the Benedictine monastery founded by St Gall, and has a population of about 75,000.

8. ROBERT EMMET (1778–1803)
Patriot, has Emmet County in the American state of Iowa named after him. The county is situated on the state's northern border with Minnesota and has a population of about 13,000.

9. EDWARD HARDMAN
Drogheda-born geologist, discovered the Kimberley gold mine; has a mountain in Western Australia named in his honour. Mount Hardman is situated about 100 miles east of the town of Broome, in the northern part of the state.

10. SAINT EVA
St Ives, the fishing port in Cornwall, England, commemorates St Eva, a fifth-century Irish woman missionary who, according to tradition, floated over from Ireland on a coracle, and was later martyred.

11. JOHN PITT KENNEDY (1796–1879)
Carndonagh, Co Donegal-born civil engineer and soldier, has an important military road in Tibet named after him, as he was responsible for its construction in 1849.

12. EARL KITCHENER of KHARTOUM
Ballylongford, Co Kerry-born field marshal, has a 150,000 population city, 50 miles south-west of Toronto, in the Canadian province of Ontario, named after him.

13. ADMIRAL SIR FRANCIS McCLINTOCK
Dundalk-born navy man famed for discovering the fate of the explorer Franklin, has a channel in northern Canada named after him. Covering an area nearly the size of Ireland, it is icebound most of the time.

14. SIR ROBERT McCLURE
Wexford-born discoverer of the North-West Passage in 1850, is remembered by the important McClure Strait, a 300 mile long by 100 mile wide stretch between Victoria Island to the south, and Melville Island to the north, in frozen north Canada.

15. JOHN MACOUN
Born Maheralin, Co Down in 1831, one of the first explorers of the Canadian Rockies, and author of *The Fauna and Flora of Canada,* has a high peak in the Rockies of Canada, and a village stop on the Canadian Pacific Railway, 200 miles west of Winnipeg, in Saskatchewan, named after him.

16. THOMAS F. MEAGHER (1823–1867)
   Young Irelander, has a big county in the American state of Montana, bigger than Ireland's second largest county, Galway, named in his honour. It is sparsely populated however, having less than one person per square mile.

17. JOHN MITCHEL (1815–1875)
   Dungiven, Co Derry-born Young Irelander and journalist, has Mitchel County, Iowa, in the United States named after him. It is situated on the state's northern boundary with Minnesota. It has a population of over 12,000 and its county town is Osage.

18. WILLIAM SMITH O'BRIEN (1803–1864)
   Repeal politician, also has a county in Iowa named after him. O'Brien County is in the north-west of the state, has a population of nearly 17,000, and has as its county seat the town of Primghar. It is nearly the same size as Co Leitrim.

19. BERNARDO O'HIGGINS (1778–1842)
   Liberator of Chile, and its first dictator, whose father, Ambrosio, a native Irishman, was Governor of Chile 1788–1795, has a province, a mountain peak, and a lake named after him in Chile. O'Higgins Province, 2,745 square miles in area, is situated just south of the capital, Santiago, and has a population of over 300,000. Lake O'Higgins, and its adjoining 2,910 metre mountain, are in the far south of Chile, on the border with Argentina.

20. SIR ARTHUR PALMER
   Premier of Queensland in Australia from 1870 to 1874; has a river named in his honour. Palmer River, which flows from the MacDonnell Range of mountains, runs south-eastwards between Alice Springs and Ayers Rock in Northern Territory, to join the River Finke. Sir Arthur was born in Co Armagh.

21. SAINT PATRICK
Commemorated on 17 March 1836, when a county in the American state of Texas, San Patricio, was named on his feast day. Bigger than Co Limerick, it has a population of about 60,000, and it incorporates some of the northern suburbs of the city of Corpus Christi.

22. ADMIRAL WILLIAM PENN
Cork-born British admiral, and father of the English Quaker-founder of the state of Pennsylvania, was honoured by King Charles II of England, by having the state his son founded named after himself. With an area of 45,333 square miles, 'Penn's Woods' (the meaning of Pennsylvania), is bigger than the island of Ireland, and is officially styled as a commonwealth.

23. ERNEST SHACKLETON
Kilkea, Co Kildare-born Antarctic explorer, has many geographical features named after him. In Antarctica, he has a glacier, an ice shelf, a section of coastline and an inlet bearing his name.

24. GENERAL JAMES SHIELDS
A Catholic and a friend of Abraham Lincoln, Shields was born in 1806 in Altmore, near Pomeroy, Co Tyrone, founded the town of Shieldville, in Minnesota, thereby encouraging Irish immigrants to move westward. Shields, on 23 March 1862, with a force of 7,000 men, badly defeated General Thomas Jonathan 'Stonewall' Jackson, at Kernstown, in the Shenandoah Valley Campaign of the American Civil War. It was to be the only time Jackson lost a military engagement.

25. THE DUKE OF WELLINGTON, Arthur Wellesley
Dublin-born conqueror of Napoleon, has many places in his honour, the chief of which is the capital city of New Zealand, Wellington, and the province of the same name in which it lies. There are also many towns etc. in England, Australia, South Africa, and the United States named after him.

Stamp of success

21 countries or territories which have honoured Irish-born people with stamps

1. ARGENTINA, in 1939 and in 1977, commemorated Foxford-born William (Guillermo) Brown, for his courage in fighting naval battles for that country against, amongst others, Spain, Brazil and France.

2. AUSTRALIA
   (a) Commemorated two Irishmen with stamps: David Collins (born in Park, Co Laois in 1756), who became Governor of Van Diemens Land (later to become Tasmania), was responsible for laying the foundation stone for the capital of the island, Hobart.
   (b) Peter Lalor (also born in Co Laois in 1823), the leader of the epoch-making events of the Eureka Stockade, and later Speaker in the Legislative Assembly of Victoria.

3. BULGARIA honoured the Bruff, Co Limerick-born *Times* war correspondent, James David Bourchier, doing so one year after he died, in 1921. He thus became the first Irishman to be honoured on a foreign stamp.

4. CANADA has commemorated 2 Irishmen on stamps.
   (a) Thomas D'Arcy Magee (born in Carlingford in 1825), for his leading example in the founding of the Canadian Confederation.
   (b) Lieutenant Colonel George French (born in 1841 in Co Roscommon), the first Commissioner of the North West Mounted Police, known today by the acronym R.C.M.P. (Royal Canadian Mounted Police).

5. CHILE, on 30 April 1970, honoured Ambrosio O'Higgins (born in Summerhill, Co Meath in 1720), a Captain-General of Chile (and later a Viceroy of Peru), with a 10 Escudos stamp.

6. THE DOMINICAN REPUBLIC honoured the Irish Olympic gold medal winner, Arklow-born Ronnie Delany, for his efforts in 1956.

7. GREAT BRITAIN commemorated Admiral Andrew Browne Cunningham (born in Dublin in 1883, died 1963), for his work as first sea lord and Commander-in-chief for the Mediterranean in the Second World War.

8. GRENADA, in the Caribbean, commemorated, on 23 November 1970, the Cork-born piratess Anne Bonny.

9. GUERNSEY, one of the Channel Islands, printed a stamp to commemorate the Roscommon-born Sir John Doyle, for his work in helping the island against the Napoleonic invasion.

10. HONDURAS, in 1981, honoured Ambrosio O'Higgins (see above), the father of Bernardo O'Higgins, who was to be 'The Liberator' of many South American countries.

11. HUNGARY commemorated the 1928 flight east to west crossing of the Atlantic with a 1978 stamp bearing portraits of Dublin-born Colonel James Fitzmaurice and his fellow aviators (G. von Hunefeld and H. Kohl).

12. INDIA, on 27 October 1968, became the first foreign country to commemorate an Irish-born woman on a stamp, when Margaret Noble (born in Dungannon, Co Tyrone in 1967), known in India as Sister Nivedita (meaning 'She who has been dedicated'), was honoured as much for her work in the independence ideal as with the poor in Calcutta.

13. The ISLE OF MAN commemorated Stanley Woods, the record breaking T.T. rider (born in Dublin in 1903).

14. KENYA issued a stamp in honour of the work of the Ballycastle, Co Down-born Bishop Donal Lamont, for his stance against apartheid in their country.

15. NORTH KOREA commemorated Ronnie Delany's winning feat in the 1,500 metres of the Melbourne Olympics of 1956 (in doing so they mis-spelt his name on the stamp).

16. RHODESIA, on 16 November 1970, issued a 15 cent stamp commemorating 'Mother Patrick' (born in Trim, Co Meath in 1863 as Mary-Ann Cosgrave), for her pioneering work in the spreading of education throughout Africa.

17. ROMANIA honoured two Irishmen on their stamps:
    (a) They marked the centenary of George Bernard Shaw's birth in November 1956 by issuing a stamp in his honour. Other East European countries have also commemorated Shaw.

    (b) Jonathan Swift was commemorated on the 300th anniversary of his birth in Dublin in 1667.

18. ST HELENA, the South Atlantic island, is the only country to honour the Duke of Wellington (born in Dublin in 1769), doing so to mark a visit by him on his way back from India.

19. TRISTAN DA CUNHA marked the 50th anniversary of the Shackleton-Rowett expedition when it issued a 12½p stamp on 1 June 1971. Sir Ernest Shackleton, the great Co Kildare-born explorer, led this endeavour.

20. The UNITED STATES honoured six Irishmen on their stamps:
    (a) A stamp was issued to honour Charles Thompson (born in Maghera, Co Derry in 1729), one of the 3 Irish-born men to sign the Declaration of Independence, his signature actually endorsing that of John Hancock, President of the Continental Congress.

    (b) John Barry (born in 1745 in Co Wexford), known in the States as 'The Father of the Navy', was remembered for his founding of that country's great naval force.

    (c) Victor Herbert, born in Dublin in 1859, appeared on a United States stamp in 1940. He was the main founder of the A.S.C.A.P., and wrote at least 40 operettas.

(d) The Dublin-born sculptor, Augustus Saint-Gaudens whose fine works include the Farragut statue in Madison Square in N.Y.C. and the Lincoln statue in Grant Park in Chicago, was also commemorated in stamp in 1940.

(e) James Hoban, the Co Kilkenny-born designer of the White House at 1600 Pennsylvania Avenue in Washington, was honoured by the United States by stamp for that accomplishment.

(f) John McCormack, the Athlone-born tenor of world-renown, has also been commemorated.

21. VENEZUELA commemorated the Cork-born (in 1801) Daniel Florence O'Leary in 1979. As an aide-de-camp for Simon Bolivar, O'Leary collected much material about him which forms the basis of modern knowledge of the great 'Liberator'.

Source: *Stamps of Success,* by Jim O'Byrne, in *Cara* magazine

WILD GEESE

If Your Name is Timothy or Pat
Irish born
52 people born in Ireland who have been
outstandingly successful in foreign countries

1. SIR JAMES AGNEW, Prime Minister of Tasmania in the 1880s, was a native of Ballyclare, Co Antrim.

2. MARIA AIKEN, British actress whose films include *A Fish Called Wanda,* was born in Dublin, 12 September 1945.

3. EARL ALEXANDER OF TUNIS, British field marshal, was born at Caledon, Co Tyrone in December 1891.

4. FRANCIS BACON, British painter, was born in Dublin on 28 October 1909.

5. LEONORA BARRY, tough United States labour leader, known as 'Mother Lake', was born in Co Cork in 1849.

6. JAMES BOURCHIER, War correspondent for *The Times* on the Balkan Peninsula, was born in Bruff, Co Limerick, 18 December 1850.

7. BRENDAN BRACKEN, politician (and confidant of Winston Churchill) and publisher, was born in Templemore, Co Tipperary in 1901.

8. WILFRED BRAMBLE, actor best known for his role as the father in the TV series *Steptoe and Son,* was born in Dublin in 1912.

9. HERBERT BRENON, 1920s film director who made *Peter Pan* and *Beau Geste,* was born in Dun Laoghaire in 1880.

10. MATHEW CAREY, prominent American publisher, was born in Dublin in 1766.

11. PETER COLLIER, founder of the United States magazine *Colliers,* was born in Myshall, Co Carlow on 12 December 1886.

12. PATRICK A. COLLINS, popular Mayor of Boston 1902–1905 (100,000 attended his funeral), was born in Fermoy in 1844.

13. PATRICK CONNOR, founder of Utah's first daily newspaper *The Union Vidette,* was born in Co Kerry in 1820.

14. RICHARD CROKER, 'Boss' of Tammany Hall in New York, was born in Clonakilty, Co Cork on 23 November 1841.

15. MARCUS DALY, the 'Copper King', a multi-millionaire, was born in Ballyjamesduff, Co Cavan in 1841.

16. CECIL DAY-LEWIS, one of 2 Irish-born poets laureate (1968–1972), was born in Ballintogher, Co Sligo in 1904.

17. WILLIAM DESMOND, silent screen star in the United States (he made over 70 movies, mostly B pictures), was born in Ireland.

18. JOHN DUNLAP, who founded the first daily paper in the United States, *The Philadelphia Packet,* was born in Strabane in 1747.

19. JAMES FAIR, millionaire miner in Nevada, who amassed $100,000,000 in 6 years, was born in Belfast, 11 December 1831.

20. BRENDAN 'PADDY' FINUCANE, British ace who downed 32 enemy planes in the Second World War, placing him fourth most successful fighter pilot, was born in Dublin, 1920.

21. THOMAS FLINN, youngest ever winner of the Victoria Cross (at 15 years and 3 months), was born in Athlone in 1842.

22. PATRICK SARSFIELD GILMORE, United States band-leader who composed *When Johnny Comes Marching Home,* was born near Dublin in December 1829.

23. CEDRIC GIBBONS (see Oscar winners), was born in Dublin on 23 March 1893.

24. WILLIAM R. GRACE, who became the first Irish-born mayor of a major American city when he was elected Mayor of New York, was born in Ireland.

25. JOHN GREGG, inventor of Gregg Shorthand, was born in Rockcorry, Co Monaghan in 1867.

26. GIANT HAYSTACKS, formidable British wrestler, was born in Ireland on 10 October 1947 under the name of Luke McMasters.

27. JOHN HUGHES, founder of Fordham University in the Bronx, New York (and New York's first archbishop),was born in Annaloghlan, Co Tipperary in 1797.

28. MARY HARRIS JONES, prominent United States labour leader known as 'Mother Jones', was born in Co Cork in 1830.

29. JIMMY KENNEDY, songwriter most famous for his *Red Sails in the Sunset,* was born in Co Tyrone, 20 July 1902.

30. DAVID LUCAS, first winner of the Victoria Cross (as a mate on HMS Helca in the Baltic he threw a live shell overboard) was born in Armagh.

31. SAM McCAUGHEY, 'The Sheep King' of Australia, who at his peak was shearing 1,000,000 sheep a year, was born in Ballymena in 1835.

32. SAMUEL McCLURE, founder of the famous muckraking magazine in the United States which bears his surname, was born in Co Antrim in 1887.

33. JOHN WILLIAM McKAY, born in Dublin in 1831, discovered the Camstock Lode in the California Gold Rush, which yielded $120,000,000 over 5 years.

34. REVEREND FRANCIS MAKAMIE, founder of the American Presbyterian Church, was a native of Ramelton, Co Donegal

35. FREDERICK MANING, 'The Pakeha Maori,' an influential worker for Maori rights in New Zealand, was born in Johnville in Dublin in 1812.

36. MIKE NOLAN, a member of the pop group Bucks Fizz, was born in Ireland on 7 December 1954.

37. AMBROSIO O'HIGGINS, Viceroy of Peru from 1795 to 1801, was born near Dangan Castle in Co Meath, in 1720.

38. WILLIAM PATTERSON, the only Irish-born United States Justice to be appointed to the Supreme Court, was born in Co Antrim in December 1745.

39. PAT PHOENIX, who became a huge hit as Elsie Tanner in *Coronation Street,* was born as Patricia Pilkington in Co Galway in 1924.

40. MICHAEL QUILL, founder of the Transport Workers Union of America, was born in Kilgarvan, Co Kerry on 18 September 1905.

41. GABRIEL READ, who extracted 112 ounces of gold in a fortnight precipitating the New Zealand Gold Rush of 1861, was born in Ireland.

42. CORNELIUS RYAN, author of *The Longest Day,* was born in Dublin on 5 June 1920.

43. AUGUSTUS SAINT-GAUDENS, American sculptor whose Adams Memorial is regarded by many as the finest sculpture in the United States, was born in Dublin, 1848.

44. GENERAL PHILIP SHERIDAN, American Civil War soldier, later Commander-in-Chief of the United States Army, was born in Co Cavan in 1831.

45. JAMES SMITH, Pennsylvanian lawyer and iron master, one of 3 Irish-born men to sign the American Declaration of Independence, was born in Dublin.

46. LAURENCE STERNE, novelist, best known for *Tristram Shandy* and *A Sentimental Journey,* was born in Clonmel in 1713.

47. WILLIAM TURNEY STEWART, dry goods store founder in the United States who left a will of $40,000,000, was born in Lisburn, Co Antrim in 1876.

48. GEORGE TAYLOR, another Pennsylvanian iron master, was one of the 3 Irish-born signatories of the American Declaration of Independence in 1776.

49. MATTHEW THORNTON, a Derry-born New Hampshire physician, was the third Irish-born person to sign the Declaration of Independence in 1776.

50. ALEXANDER WALKER, film critic with the *London Evening Standard,* was born in Northern Ireland on 22 March 1930.

51. JOHN WALKER, founder of the Church of God in the United States, was born in Co Roscommon in 1833.

52. REBECCA WEST, British writer and journalist, was born in Co Kerry in 1892, as Cicely Isobel Fairfield.

---

and ... 3 born at sea!

---

1. SEAMUS McCALL (1892–1964), biographer and historian, best known for his *Thomas Moore* (1935), and *Irish Mitchel* (1937), was born at sea. As a schoolboy, he ran away to South America, getting work on the first railway line to cross the Andes.

2. EDWARD MacLYSAGHT (1887–1986), the genealogist, was born to a Clare family, while they were en route to Australia, on 6 November 1887. He wrote many works on Irish surnames and their origins during his career, spending many years as Chief Genealogical Officer and Keeper of Manuscripts at the National Library.

3. LADY MORGAN (c 1775–1859), the novelist (real name Sydney Owenson), was supposedly born at sea, although there is some evidence that she was born in Dublin in 1780 or 1783. She became a society lady, and her best known novels are *St Clair,* and *The Wild Irish Girl.* Her travel books were also famous.

Second Generation
16 famous people with Irish parents

1. JIM BRADDOCK
   World Heavyweight Boxing Champion from 1935 to 1937. His parents, although they had spent a number of years in Mottram in Lancashire before emigrating to the United States, were in fact both from Ireland.

2. ELLEN BURSTYN
   Actress, won an Oscar for her portrayal of the role of Alice Hyatt in the film *Alice Doesn't Live Here Anymore;* born of Irish parents in 1932 with the real name of Edna Gilhooly.

3. 'GENTLEMAN JIM' CORBETT
   World Heavyweight Boxing Champion 1892–1897; father from Shrule, near Tuam, in Galway, mother from Dublin.

4. PATRICK DUFFY
   Actor, played *The Man from Atlantis,* and the role of Bobby Ewing in *Dallas* on TV; was born on St Patrick's Day 1949, the son of Tony and Marie Duffy, both of whom were killed during a raid on their business in 1987.

5. JOHN FINCHLEY DUNNE
   Humorist; created the inimitable character of Martin Dooley, who had an enormous influence on the political and public thinking of America in the early twentieth century; born of immigrant Irish parents.

6. BOY GEORGE
   Pop singer, formerly with Culture Club; born in London on 14 June 1961, the son of Irish immigrants from Co Tipperary.

7. HENRY FORD
   Founder of the Ford Corporation of America; born in Dearborn, Michigan in 1863, of parents, John and Thomasina Ford, who had emigrated to the United States 23 years previously after being evicted from a holding in Co Cork.

8. JOHN HEENAN
   Cardinal and eighth Archbishop of Westminster; born to staunch Irish Catholic parents in Ilford, on 26 January 1905.

9. THOMAS LIPTON
   Wealthy tea merchant, philanthropist, and Americas Cup yachtsman; born on 10 May 1850 to Irish parents who ran a grocery shop in Glasgow.

10. JOHN McCLOSKEY
    First United States Cardinal; born in Brooklyn, New York in 1810, the son of recently arrived Irish mother and father.

11. BRIAN MULRONEY
    Prime Minister of Canada since 1984; son of parents from Co Cavan.

12. THOMAS A. MURPHY
    Chairman of General Motors Corporation from 1974; son of Irish parents.

13. PAT O'BRIEN
    Hollywood actor, best known for his roles in *The Front Page, Angels With Dirty Faces,* and *Boy Meets Girl;* born in Milwaukee, Wisconsin on 11 November 1899 of Irish parents.

14. LEONORA O'REILLY
    United States labour leader; born to parents from Ireland, on 16 February 1870.

15. JOHN L. SULLIVAN
    World Heavyweight Boxing Champion for 10 years 1882–1892, known as the Boston Strong Boy; father from Tralee, Co Kerry, mother from Athlone, Co Westmeath.

16. GENE TUNNEY
    World Heavyweight boxing champion from 1926 to 1928; the son of parents from Kiltimagh in Co Mayo.

    PS: MUHAMMAD ALI, 3 times boxing's World Heavyweight Champion (1964–1967, 1974–1977, and in 1979), had a grandfather from his mother's side of the family, who was an O'Grady from Co Clare.

Mother's Pride
16 famous people who had an Irish mother

1. HILAIRE BELLOC
   French writer, born in St Cloud, France in July 1870; was the son of the Irish suffragette Bessie Rayner Parkes.

2. WILLIAM BONEY ('BILLY THE KID')
   American outlaw, was the son of an Irish mother, Catherine. He was shot dead by another Irish-American, Pat Garret, 15 July 1881.

3. JUANITA CASEY
   Writer, born to an Irish tinker mother, Annie Moloney, 10 October 1925, in England. Her mother died giving birth to her.

4. RAYMOND CHANDLER
   Creator of Philip Marlowe in such classics as *Farewell My Lovely* and *The Big Sleep;* his mother (a Thornton) was from Waterford. He spent many summers as a child at the home of his uncle Ernest Thornton in Thomastown, Co Waterford.

5. CHARLIE CHAPLIN
   Comedian and film-maker, born 15 April 1889 in London, to an Irish mother from Cork called Hannah Hill.

6. WALT DISNEY
   Creator of Mickey Mouse and Donald Duck, and of Disneyland; born to an Irish-born mother, Mary Richardson, in Chicago, Illinois, 5 December 1905.

7. HARRISON FORD
   Star of the 3 *Star Wars* films, and the 3 *Indiana Jones* movies; was born to an Irish Catholic mother in Chicago, Illinois, 13 July 1942.

8. JOHN FRANKENHEIMER
   Film director best known for *The Manchurian Candidate, The Birdman of Alcatraz* and *French Connection II,* was born to an Irish mother 19 February 1930 in New York.

9. ULYSSES S. GRANT
   Hero of the American Civil War and the 18th President of the United States; born at Point Pleasant, Clermont County, Ohio, 27 April 1822, to Harriet Simpson, from Derigna in Northern Ireland. The S. in his surname stands for Simpson, after his mother's maiden name.

10. ALFRED HITCHCOCK
    Director of such major films as *Psycho, Suspicion, Rear Window* and *The Birds;* born in London 13 August 1899 to Emma Whelan from Cork.

11. ANNE JACKSON
    Actress, born in Allegheny, Pennsylvania on 3 September 1926 to an Irish mother. Her best film roles include *The Secret Life of an American Wife* and *Lovers and Other Strangers.*

12. KEVIN KLINE
    Actor of stage and screen, noted for his roles in *The Big Chill, Sophie's Choice* and *A Fish Called Wanda;* born to an Irish Catholic mother whose maiden name was Delaney, in St Louis, Missouri, on 24 October 1947

13. ANGELA LANSBURY
    Famous for her TV role as Jessica Fletcher in *Murder She Wrote,* but also an accomplished film and stage actress; is the daughter of the actress, Moya McGill, who was born in Belfast on 10 December 1895.

14. OLIVIA MANNING
    Author of *The Balkan Trilogy;* born 2 March 1908, the daughter of a woman from Co Down. Her early work, *Winds of Change,* was set in Dublin.

15. GUIGLIELMO MARCONI
    Inventor, born in Bologna, Italy 25 April 1884; his mother was the daughter of Andrew Jameson of Co Wexford.

16. MARTIN SHEEN
    Hollywood actor, born as Ramon Estevez in Dayton, Ohio on 8 March 1940, to a Spanish immigrant father, Francisco Estevez, and a mother from Borrisokane, Co Tipperary, Mary Ann Phelan. He is the father of the up-and-coming actors, Emilio Estevez, and Charlie Sheen.

The Male Line
20 famous people who had an Irish father

1. CHESTER ALAN ARTHUR
   The 21st President of the United States was the son of a Reverend William Arthur who emigrated from Dreen, near Ballymena in 1806.

2. ANNE, CHARLOTTE and EMILY BRONTË
   The writers from the Haworth Parsonage were all daughters of a Co Down-born clergyman, Patrick Brontë, born there in 1777.

3. JAMES BUCHANAN
   The 15th President of the United States was the son of an Irishman of the same name from Ramelton, Co Donegal, who emigrated to the United States in 1783, and who died on 11 June 1821.

4. JAMES CAGNEY
   Actor and dancer; the son of an Irish New York bartender.

5. MADELINE CARROLL
   Actress, best known for her part as the perfect foil for Robert Donat in Alfred Hitchcock's *The 39 Steps;* born with a great Limerick name of Marie O'Connell, as it was there that her father was born.

6. GEORGE CLINTON
   Born 26 July 1739, the son of an emigrant from Longford who emigrated 10 years earlier. Became Vice-President of the United States in the administrations of Thomas Jefferson and James Madison, and was the first Governor of New York State.

7. PHIL DONAGHUE
   American talk-show host; is the son of a Catholic Irish furniture salesman, and was born in Cleveland, Ohio on 21 December 1935.

8. 'WILD BILL' DONOVAN
Founder of the OSS (the forerunner to the CIA) in the United States; was born to a Cork-born father on New Year's Day in 1883.

9. GENERAL REGINALD EDWARD HARRY DYER
Brigadier-general in command of the notorious slaughter in Amritsar in April 1919; although born in Murree in the Punjab in 1864, was the son of an Irish brewer, and attended school at Midleton College, Mullingar.

10. ROBERT GRAVES
British poet and novelist, famous for his autobiography *Goodbye To All That,* and his historical novels, *I Claudius* and *Claudius The God;* was the son of the Irish-born poet, Alfred Perceval Graves (1846–1931).

11. PAUL HOGAN
Australian film star best known for his *Crocodile Dundee* roles in 2 hit films; was born 8 October 1939 in Lightning Ridge, New South Wales, to an Irish Catholic father.

12. ANDREW JACKSON
The seventh President of the United States was born in 1767 after his father, Andrew Jackson, had died, less than 2 years after emigrating with his mother from Carrickfergus.

13. BOBBY LOCKE
South African-born golfer, won the British Open Championship title 4 times, in 1949, 1950, 1952 and 1957; was the son of a Belfast man.

14. NED KELLY
Australian bushranger of the outback; was the son of John 'Red' Kelly, a Tipperary-born convict deported to Australia for stealing 2 pigs in Ireland.

15. SIMON KENTON
American frontiersman and Indian fighter; was the son of an Irishman who emigrated to the United States.

16. JUAN O'GORMAN
    One of Mexico's most accomplished twentieth-century architects; born on 6 July 1905 to an Irish father and a Mexican mother.

17. BERNARDO O'HIGGINS (1778–1842)
    First dictator of the new regime in Chile in 1817–1823; son of a Co Meath-born politician, Ambrosio O'Higgins, himself a Viceroy of Peru.

18. EUGENE O'NEILL
    America's greatest twentieth-century playwright, whose major works include *The Iceman Cometh, A Long Day's Journey into Night, Mourning Becomes Electra,* and *Emperor Jones;* was the son of an enormously popular Kilkenny-born actor, James O'Neill.

19. ANTHONY QUINN
    Star of *Lust for Life, The Guns of Navarone, Zorba the Greek* and *The Shoes of the Fisherman;* born in the Mexican province of Chihuahua on 21 April 1915, the son of an Irishman by the name of Frank Quinn.

20. SIR ARTHUR SULLIVAN
    Famous for the comic operettas written in conjunction with W.S. Gilbert, such as *The Pirates of Penzance, The MIkado, HMS Pinafore* and *The Gondoliers;* the son of an Irish musician/bandmaster at the Sandhurst Royal Military College. His mother, although bearing the maiden name of Mary Coghlan, was of Italian descent.

High Flyers
16 United States Presidents of Irish descent

1. JAMES MONROE
   The 5th President. Descended from an old family who took their name from Mount Roe near Limavaddy, Co Derry. In the 17th century, an Andrew Monroe was serving as a major under the kinsman Sir George Munroe, Governor of Coleraine. He was banished to Virginia as a Loyalist, and there founded the family from whom James Monroe was born at Westmoreland County, Virginia, in 1758.

2. ANDREW JACKSON
   The 7th President was the son of Irish immigrants. His father, also Andrew Jackson, who died before he was born, was a linen worker from Carrickfergus who emigrated in 1765 with his wife, Elizabeth Hutchinson. He is said officially to have been born in South Carolina on 15 March 1767. However, Allan W. Eckert, in his book, *The Frontiersman,* contends that he was in fact born in 1755 on an emigrant ship bound for the United States from Ireland. (His evidence includes a woman who claims to have delivered him.)

3. JAMES KNOX POLK
   The 11th President. Born in North Carolina iin 1795, was the son of a farmer and surveyor of Scots-Irish descent, Samuel Polk, who emigrated to America in 1783. Polk's great-great-grandfather, William Polk, was born in Co Donegal in 1664.

4. DAVID RICHE ATCHISON
   The son of an Irishman. As he was president *pro tempore* of the United States Senate, on 4 March 1849 became President for the day. At midnight of 3 March, President Polk went out of office; because his successor Zachary Taylor refused to be inaugurated on a Sunday, the office fell to Atchison for that one day, making him the shortest holder of the role.

5. ANDREW JOHNSON
   The 17th President, whose ancestry is a mixture of Irish, English and Scots, was born in 1808 in Raleigh, North Carolina. His grandfather, a small farmer, emigrated to America from Ballyeaston near Larne, Co Antrim, around 1750.

6. ULYSSES S. GRANT
   The 18th President had strong Irish ancestry on his mother's side. Harriet Simpson was the granddaughter of James Simpson, who emigrated from Derigna near Ballygawley, Co Tyrone as a young man in 1738.

7. CHESTER ALAN ARTHUR
   The 21st President was the son of Reverend William Arthur, who had emigrated to the United States in 1806, having been born at Dreen (meaning 'place of the thorns') near Ballymena in 1796. The family home in the eartly 19th century was at Cullybackey, Co Antrim.

8. GROVER CLEVELAND
   President from 1885 to 1889 and again from 1893 to 1897. Was born in Caldwell, New Jersey, on 18 March 1837, of a mixture of English and Scots-Irish descent.

9. WILLIAM McKINLEY
   The 25th President had Irish ancestors on the paternal side who emigrated to the American colonies at the end of the 17th century. His great-great-grandfather came from Ballymoney, Co Antrim, and went to America in the mid 1700s. His own grandfather, James McKinley, was born in 1783 at Conacher's Farm, at Dervock, Co Antrim.

10. WILLIAM HOWARD TAFT
    The 27th President, who served from 1909 to 1913, was born in Cincinnati on 15 September 1857, of English and Scots-Irish descent.

11. WOODROW WILSON
    The 28th President was of Scots-Irish descent, his grandfather, James Wilson, having emigrated to Philadelphia in 1807 from Strabane, Co Tyrone. His grandmother, Amy Adams, came from the Sion Mills area of Co Tyrone.

12. WARREN G. HARDING
    The 29th President. Born at Blooming Grove, Ohio on 2 November 1865, into a family which had an English and Scots-Irish background. He was President for only 2 and a half years, dying in office in August 1923.

13. HARRY S. TRUMAN
    President from 1945 to 1949, was of Scots-Irish and English extraction.

14. JOHN F. KENNEDY
    The 35th President was perhaps the most Irish of all Presidents, as all his ancestry can be traced to Ireland. His great-grandfather was born in Dunganstown, Co Wexford in 1823, and emigrated to America in 1840 at the age of 17, settling in the Boston area.

15. RICHARD NIXON
    The 37th President comes from a Leinster Quaker background. His great-great-great-great-grandfather, James Nixon, emigrated from Ireland to Delaware in 1731.

16. RONALD REAGAN
    The 40th President, 1981–1989, has strong Irish connections. In 1858, his great-grandparents, Michael and Catherine Reagan emigrated to Fairhaven, Illinois, from a townland near Ballyporeen, Co Tipperary.

6 Australian Prime Ministers of Irish descent

During the important period of growth in Australian history between 1929 and 1949, 6 of its 7 Prime Ministers in the period were of close Irish descent. They were:

1. JAMES A. SCULLIN (1876–1953)
   Prime Minister (for the Labour Party) from October 1929 to 1932 during the period of the Depression; was born, of Irish descent, on 28 January 1870. He died in January 1953.

2. JOSEPH A. LYONS (1879–1939)
   Succeeded Scullin to the highest office in 1932, was in charge of the country's affairs during a period of great growth. Lasted in office until 1939. He was born in Tasmania of Irish stock on 15 September 1879, and died in office on 17 April 1939.

3. ARTHUR W. FADDEN (1895–1973)
   Prime Minister for a brief period in war-time, 1941; of Irish descent. His effort to form a stable government failed and he was defeated after only 5 weeks in office.

4. JOHN JOSEPH CURTIN (1885–1945)
   Probably the most influential of the 6 Prime Ministers of Irish descent to hold office. Held the post for most of the Second World War, and acquitted himself well in the job. During office he introduced a measure of conscription, and pushed for Australia's right to be consulted on the way the war was being conducted in the Pacific. He was born (the son of a Corkman) on 8 January 1885 in Creswick, Victoria. From being a secretary of the Victoria branch of the Timber Workers' Union he went on to become the leader of the Labor Party in opposition for 6 years before taking power in 1941. He died in office just before the end of the war.

5. FRANCIS M. FORDE (1890–1983)
Born of Irish stock, held the position at the head of government for a week, in a caretaker capacity, in 1945, after the death of John Curtin

6. JOSEPH BENEDICT CHIFLEY (1885–1951)
Last of the Irish-descended Prime Ministers; born in New South Wales on 22 September 1885. A close colleague of John Curtin, he was a Member of the House of Representatives (MHR), and of the war cabinet during the Second World War. He served as Prime Minister for 4 difficult years after the end of the war, until 1949. He died in 1951 while still in opposition.

3 Irish-born New Zealand Prime Ministers

1. JOHN EDWARD FITZGERALD
New Zealand's first Prime Minister was born in Ireland.

2. JOHN BALLANCE
Born near Lough Neagh in Glenavy, Co Antrim in March 1839, the son of a Quaker farmer, emigrated as a young man of 26 to New Zealand. He later became Prime Minister in the Liberal interest and died in office in 1893, having served for 12 years. In office he made major tax reforms, land ownership changes, and was instrumental in introducing women's suffrage into New Zealand.

3. WILLIAM FERGUSON MASSEY
Prime Minister of New Zealand for 13 years from 1912 to 1925; born in Limavady, Co Derry in 1856, the son of a small farm holder. Having emigrated to farm in New Zealand in 1870, he later became a Member of the House of Representatives (MHR). He led the opposition party (Conservative) for 8 years before being made Prime Minister in 1912, and formed a National Government in 1915.

Canada

SIR FRANCIS HICKS
Premier of Canada for 3 years; was born in Cork in 1807, later emigrating to Canada and setting up a business in Toronto. After his period as premier (from 1851 to 1854), he was made Governor of Barbados and the Windward Islands, and later of British Guiana. Later still he was made Minister for Finance in the government of John MacDonald, 1869–1873. Some time after, he survived a banking scandal, and died in August 1885.

United Kingdom

THE FIRST DUKE OF WELLINGTON
Born Arthur Wellesley in Mornington House in Merrion Street Dublin on 29 April 1769; apart from being the hero of Waterloo, was the only Irish-born British Prime Minister. He held the office from 1828 until 1830, when he was replaced by Earl Grey. During his time in office, he passed Catholic Emancipation, but his total opposition to parliamentary reform made his term very unpopular.

THE WEARING OF
THE GREEN

Gift of Citizenship
Ireland's 6 Honorary Citizens

1. Chester Beatty
2. Jack Charlton
3 and 4. Tieda Herrema and his wife Elizabeth
5 and 6. Tip O'Neill and his wife Mildred

Miscarriages of Justice
'The Guildford Four'

1.	Gerard Conlon, sentenced 30 years
2.	Carol Richardson, indefinite sentence
3.	Patrick Armstrong, 35 year sentence
4.	Paul Hill, indefinite sentence

'The Birmingham Six'

1.	John Walker	4.	William Power
2.	Noel Richard McIlhenny	5.	Patrick Joseph Hill
3.	Hugh Callaghan	6.	Robert Gerard Hunter

Honorary Consuls
'The Four Horsemen'

Nickname of 4 Irish-Americans who led in the effort to highlight the problems of Northern Ireland to Americans

1.   Governor Hugh Carey of New York

2.   Senator Edward Kennedy of Massachusetts

3.   Speaker of the House of Representatives, Tip O'Neill

4.   New York Senator Daniel Patrick Moynihan

Outsiders
Well known Irish people not born in Ireland

1. PIARAS BEASLAI, 1916 fighter and writer, was born in Liverpool in 1881.

2. CHESTER BEATTY, philanthropist and art collector, Ireland's first ever Honorary Citizen, was born in New York in 1875.

3. REBECCA BEST, Ireland's No. 1 squash player, reaching a ranking in the world's top 10, was born in Lancashire, to Irish parents, in 1965.

4. PAULINE BEWICK, Irish painter, was born in Northumberland in 1935.

5. ERSKINE CHILDERS, fourth President of Ireland, was born in London in 1905.

6. ERSKINE CHILDERS, father of the above, revolutionary, and author of *The Riddle of the Sands,* was also born in London.

7. THOMAS CLARKE, one of the 7 signatories of the 1916 Proclamation, was born on the Isle of Wight in 1857.

8. ADAM CLAYTON, bass guitarist of the rock group U2, was born in Chinoor, Oxfordshire to British parents.

9. JAMES CONNOLLY, Irish socialist and leader of the 1916 Rising, for which he was executed, was born in 1868 in the Edinburgh slum of Cowgate.

10. JEREMIAH CURTIN, collector of Irish fairytales, was born, to Irish parents, in Detroit, Michigan, in 1835.

11. CYRIL CUSACK, Ireland's premier actor in modern times, was born near Durban in South Africa in 1910.

12. CHRIS de BURGH, Irish singer and songwriter, was born on a farm near Buenos Aires in 1957.

13. JOHN de COURCY IRELAND, authority on Irish maritime affairs, was born in Lucknow, India in 1911.

14. EAMON de VALERA, revolutionary of 1916 and 1922 and Taoiseach and President of Ireland, was born in Manhattan, New York in 1882.

15. MATT DOYLE, Ireland's Davis Cup and Kings Cup player, was born in Redwood City, California in 1955.

16. TOMMY DOYLE, winner of 7 All-Ireland SFC medals with Kerry between 1978 and 1986, was born in New York.

17. LOUISE GAVAN DUFFY, founder of Scoil Bride, and revolutionary, was born in Nice in Italy in 1884.

18. MARIA EDGEWORTH, Irish novelist, was born in Black Bourton in Oxfordshire in 1767.

19. HILTON EDWARDS, actor–producer and partner of Micheal Mac Liammoir, was born in London on 2 February 1903.

20. DAVE EVANS, 'The Edge', U2's lead guitarist, was born in Barking Hospital in East London, to Welsh parents, in 1961.

21. BRIAN FARRELL, *Today Tonight* RTE presenter, and lecturer in politics, was born in Manchester in 1929.

22. THEODORA FITZGIBBON, cookery expert and writer, was born in London to Irish parents in 1916.

23. VERE FOSTER, educationalist and philanthropist, was born in Copenhagen, Denmark in 1819.

24. TONY GALVIN, one of the Republic of Ireland's soccer team which excelled in Germany in 1988, was born in Huddersfield.

25. JAMES GANDON, architect of the Custom House and the Four Courts in Dublin, was born in London in 1743.

26. THOMAS JOHNSON, first leader of the Labour Party in parliamentary affairs, was born in Liverpool in 1872.

27. WILLIAM JOYCE, 'Lord Haw Haw', the Irishman who broadcast for the Nazis from wartime Germany, was born in New York in about 1906.

28. 'BIG JIM' LARKIN, charismatic labour leader and founder of the ITGWU, was born in Liverpool in 1876.

29. MARY LAVIN, Irish writer, was born in East Walpole, Massachusetts in 1912.

30. EDDIE McATEER, former Nationalist Party leader of Northern Ireland, was born in Coatbridge, Scotland in 1914.

31. CATALINA MacBRIDE, revolutionary and wife of Sean MacBride, was born in Buenos Aires in 1901.

32. MAUD GONNE MacBRIDE, revolutionary, was born in Aldershot, England in 1865.

33. SEAN MacBRIDE, Nobel Prize-winner was born in Paris in 1904, the son of Maud Gonne and the 1916 leader, John MacBride.

34. EUGENE McCABE, Northern Irish writer, noted for his TV trilogy on the Troubles, was born in Glasgow in 1923.

35. SHANE McGOWAN, lead singer with The Pogues, was born in England in 1957, when his parents were on holiday there.

36. PHILIP MATTHEWS, Irish rugby wing forward and captain, was born in Gloucestershire in 1960.

37. BARBARA MULLEN, Irish actress best known for her role as the housekeeper in TV's *Dr Finlay's Casebook,* was born in Boston, Massachusetts.

38. BRENDAN MULLIN, Irish and Lions centre three-quarter rugby player, was born in Israel in 1963.

39. MICHAEL J. MURPHY, writer and collector of Irish folk tales, was born in Liverpool in 1913, his parents being from South Armagh.

40. DAVID NORRIS, Senator, Civil Liberties and Gay Rights advocate, was born in Leopoldville in the Congo in 1944.

41. SEAN O'hEIGHEARTAIGH, publisher, was born in Welshpool, Wales in 1917.

42. TOM PAULIN, Northern Irish poet, was born in Leeds in 1949.

43. SIR HORACE PLUNKETT, who pioneered the phenomenon of agricultural co-operatives in Ireland, was born in Gloucestershire in 1854.

44. ARTHUR POWER, writer and painter, and friend of James Joyce, was born in Guernsey in 1891.

45. HAMILTON ROWAN, United Irishman, was born in London on 12 May 1751.

46. MICHAEL SMURFIT, head of the multinational Smurfit organisation was born in St Helens, Lancashire in 1936.

47. R.M. SMYLLIE, editor of the *Irish Times* from 1934 to 1954, was born in Glasgow in 1894.

48. EDITH SOMERVILLE, the longer-surviving of the Somerville and Ross writing partnership, was born in Corfu in 1858.

49. ADRIAN STOKES, Irish pathologist, was born in Lausanne, Switzerland in 1887.

50. FRANCIS STUART, Irish writer, was born in Queensland, Australia in 1902.

51. MICHAEL VINEY, journalist and writer, was born in Brighton in 1934.

52. JACK BUTLER YEATS, painter and younger brother of William Butler Yeats, was born in London in 1871.

53. JIMMY MAGEE, popular sports commentator, was born in the Bronx, New York.

ENTERTAINERS

1. CEDRIC GIBBONS
   Dublin-born art director; regarded as one of the most influential production designers in the history of American films. He designed the Academy Award statuette in 1927. A secretary said of it, 'It reminds me of my uncle Oscar'. The rest is history. Gibbons himself went on to be nominated innumerable times, and actually won 12 Oscars, listed below:
   (i)   *The Bridge of San Luis Rey* (1929)
   (ii)   *The Merry Widow* (1934)
   (iii)   *Pride and Prejudice* (1940)
   (iv)   *Blossoms in the Dust* (1941)
   (v)   *Gaslight* (1944)
   (vi)   *The Yearling* (1946)
   (vii)   *Little Women* (1949)
   (viii) An honorary Oscar for 'consistent excellence' (1950)
   (ix)   *An American in Paris* (1951)
   (x)   *The Bad and the Beautiful* (1952)
   (xi)   *Julius Caesar* (1953)
   (xii)   *Somebody Up There Likes Me* (1956)

2. BARRY FITZGERALD
   Born William Shields in Dublin; won the Best Supporting Actor for his role as the crotchety old pastor in the New York slum parish, Father Fitzgibbon, in *Going My Way*. He was also nominated for Best Actor for the same role. Bing Crosby won the main award, and later presented his statuette to the Irish-born Father Flanagan, of 'Boy's Town' fame.

3. GEORGE BERNARD SHAW
   Dublin-born playwright; won an Academy Award for the 1938 film version of 'Pygmalion' (*My Fair Lady*), making him the only person in history to win both an Oscar and a Nobel Prize for Literature. He did not, however, accept the award, remarking, as he did about all awards, 'I've been offered titles, but they get one into disreputable company.'

4. GREER GARSON
   Co Down-born Hollywood leading lady of the 1940s and 1950s; won a Best Actress Oscar for playing the title role as the indomitable English housewife who survives the Second World War, in William Wyler's *Mrs Miniver*. This was her only Oscar win in 7 monimations as Best Actress, from 1939 to 1960.

5. JOSIE McAVIN
   Dublin-born Art Director; twice nominated in the 1960s, finally won the Academy Award she deserved in 1985 for her magnificent work in Sidney Pollack's *Out of Africa*, the story of Karen Blixen.

6. MICHELE BURKE
   Shared with Sarah Monzani, in 1982, the Academy Award for Best Make-Up for her work on the Jean-Jacques Annaud film *Quest for Fire*, a film about a primitive tribe's discovery that fire can be used to defeat enemies. Winning in the face of stiff competition from *Gandhi* (a multi-award winner that year), *Quest for Fire's* Oscar was well received.

Irish Oscar Nominees

Below is a list of Irish people who have been honoured with an Academy Award nomination, but who have failed to win the actual statuette.

1939 GERALDINE FITZGERALD, for her role as Isabella Linton in William Wyler's classic film version of Emily Brontë's *Wuthering Heights*, received a Best Supporting Actress Academy Award nomination.

1939   GREER GARSON, the Co Down-born actress, won her first Best Actress nomination for portraying Mrs Chipping opposite the Oscar-winning performance of Richard Donat in the Sam Wood-directed version of *Goodbye Mr Chips*.

1941   GREER GARSON, for her role as Mrs Edna Gladney in the film *Blossoms in the Dust* received her second Best Actress nomination.

1941   SARA ALLGOOD, sister of the Irish actress Molly Allgood, won a Best Supporting Actress nomination for portraying the mother in the mining family in the John Ford classic, *How Green Was My Valley*.

1941   PATRICIA COLLINGE, the Dublin-born actress, received a nomination for Best Supporting Actress for her role as Aunt Bridie Hubbert in *Little Foxes*.

1943   GREER GARSON, for portraying the lead role of the Polish-born scientist Marie Curie in the film *Madame Curie,* won her fourth Best Actress nomination (her third, the previous year, leading her to win; see Oscar winners).

1944   BARRY FITZGERALD (see Oscar winners) was nominated for Best Actor for the same role in which he won the Best Supporting Actor Academy Award in *Going My Way*.

1944   GREER GARSON won her fifth nomination for Best Actress with her portrayal of the title role in a low-quality drama, *Mrs Parkington*.

1945   GREER GARSON won her fifth Best Actress nomination in five consecutive years (and her sixth in seven years) when named for the lead role in *Valley of Decision*.

1949   RICHARD TODD, in only his second film, won a Best Actor nomination for his role as an angry young Scot in an army hospital in Burma who finds out he is going to die, in *The Hasty Heart*.

1953 DAN O'HERLIHY, the Wexford-born Irish actor, was nominated for portraying the title role in the 1953 Luis Buñuel film version of the Daniel Defoe novel, *The Adventures of Robinson Crusoe*.

1960 GREER GARSON won her seventh and last Oscar nomination, all for Best Actress, playing the role of Eleanor Roosevelt, wife of the United States President, in *Sunrise at Campobello*.

1962 PETER O'TOOLE won his first Best Actor nomination in his first major starring role, as T.E. Lawrence in David Lean's epic, *Lawrence of Arabia*.

1963 RICHARD HARRIS, the Limerick-born actor, won his only Oscar nomination, received for Best Actor, in his sensitive portrayal of Frank Machin in the film version of the Peter Storey book, *This Sporting Life*.

1963 JOSIE McAVIN, the set designer, won her first Academy Award nomination for her work on the Tony Richardson film of the Henry Fielding novel, *Tom Jones*.

1964 PETER O'TOOLE won his second Best Actor nomination for playing King Henry II opposite Richard Burton's title role in *Beckett,* directed by Peter Grenville.

1965 JOSIE McAVIN won her unsuccessful Oscar nomination for her fine, bleak set design of the Martin Ritt film of the John Le Carré novel, *The Spy Who Came In From The Cold*.

1968 PETER O'TOOLE received his third Best Actor nomination for playing (for the second time in a nominated role, a rare feat) King Henry II opposite Katherine Hepburn's Oscar-winning performance as Eleanor of Aquitaine, in *The Lion in Winter*.

1969 PETER O'TOOLE'S role in the otherwise fairly ordinary treatment of James Hilton's *Goodbye Mr Chips* won him a deserved fourth Oscar nomination for Best Actor, failing on this occasion to John Wayne's Oscar for *True Grit*.

1972 PETER O'TOOLE, playing the anarchic Jack, son of the Earl of Gurney in *The Ruling Class,* won his fifth Best Actor nomination.

1974 LOUIS MARCUS won a Best Documentary nomination in 1974 for *Paisti Ag Obair* (*Children At Work*) which was filmed for Gael Linn in three Montessori schools.

1976 LOUIS MARCUS won his second nomination for Best Documentary in this year for his film about the making of Waterford Glass, *Conquest of Light.*

1980 PETER O'TOOLE won his sixth Academy Award nomination for Best Actor with his leading role in the melodrama of Paul Brodeur's novel, *The Stunt Man.*

1982 PETER O'TOOLE received his seventh Best Actor nomination for a brilliantly comic performance as Allan Swann in Richard Benjamin's romp, *My Favourite Year.* This total of seven nominations for a leading role in a film places him in the unenviable position of being the most nominated actor never to receive an Academy Award!

Chart toppers
Ireland's only singles to make No. 1 in Britain

1. RUBY MURRAY with *SOFTLY, SOFTLY* (Columbia DB 3558).
As a 19-year-old, she became the most successful singer in the British charts in 1955. This song became No. 1 in February of that year, and remained there for 3 weeks. It was written by Mark Paul and Pierre Dudan; lyrics by Paddy Roberts. It was to be Ruby Murray's only No. 1 hit.

2. THE BATCHELORS with *DIANE* (Decca F 11799)
These three affable married men from Dublin, were enormously popular in 1963–1964. Con Cluskey, Declan Cluskey and John Stokes reached No. 1 in February

1964, staying there for only one week. The song was produced by Michael Barclay, and was written by Erno Rapee and Lew Pollack.

3. DANA with *ALL KINDS OF EVERYTHING* (Rex 11054)
   Rosemary Brown, her real name, had recently become the toast of Europe with this song, a popular winner of the 1970 Eurovision Song Contest. Written by Denny Lindsay and Jackie Smith, and produced by Ray Herricks, the song became No. 1 in April, and stayed there for 2 weeks.

4. GILBERT O'SULLIVAN with *CLAIR* (Mam 84)
   Born in Waterford as Raymond O'Sullivan, and became noted for his outrageous attire; he reached No. 1 with this ballad in November 1972, and remained there for 2 weeks. Written by the singer himself, the Clair in the title refers to the infant daughter of his manager, Gordon Mills, who produced the record.

5. GILBERT O'SULLIVAN with *GET DOWN* (Mam 96)
   Made him the first Irish person to have had two No. 1 hits in the British charts. His *Alone Again* climbed to No. 3 and reached No. 1 in the United States. *Get Down* was also written by the singer, and produced by Gordon Mills, and became No. 1 for 2 weeks in April 1973.

6. THE BOOMTOWN RATS with *RAT TRAP* (Ensign ENY 16)
   Regarded as the first 'New Wave' No. 1, this song by the Dublin group was the third 'A' side to be released from the album *Tonic for the Troops*. Written by Bob Geldof, it was 4 minutes long, and was 2 weeks at No. 1 in November 1978.

7. THE BOOMTOWN RATS with *I DON'T LIKE MONDAYS* (Ensign ENY 30).
   Written by Bob Geldof after hearing a news report about a teenage Californian schoolgirl who became a sniper and killed some of her classmates, the title being her reported reply as to why she committed the atrocity. Produced by Phil Wainman, the song was not a hit in the United States, but was 2 weeks at the top spot in Britain, in July 1979.

8. JOHNNY LOGAN with *WHAT'S ANOTHER YEAR* (Epic EPC 8572)
   Winner of the recent Eurovision Song Contest, the song reached the top of the British charts in May 1980. Written by Shay Healy, and produced by Bill Whelan and Dave Pennefeather, it came in and went out of the charts so quickly, that despite staying at the top for 2 weeks, it has the unenviable record of having the shortest time of any British No. 1 in the charts.

9. FEARGAL SHARKEY with *A GOOD HEART*
   Derryman Sharkey, a former lead singer with The Undertones, reached his career peak with this popular song, which reached No. 1 in November 1985, and remained there for 2 weeks.

10. CHRIS de BURGH with *THE LADY IN RED*
    After many years of writing and singing excellent middle-of-the-road songs, this Argentina-born Irishman finally got the big break with this tribute to his wife. It reached No. 1 in July 1986, and remained there for 4 weeks, making it the longest stay for an Irish single at the top of the prestigious British charts.

11. U2 with *DESIRE*
    Off their *Rattle and Hum* album.

12. ENYA with *ORINOCO FLOW*. Taken off her album *Watermark*, this untypical hit song proved enormously popular in 1988 and set Enya off on a successful career.

THE SPORTING LIFE

Olympic Champions
22 Irish winners of Olympic gold medals

The Republic of Ireland have won only 4 gold medals in the Olympic Games. However, a total of 22 Irish sports persons have won Olympic golds, for such diverse countries as Canada, South Africa, the United Kingdom and, of course, the United States. They are listed below:

1. TIM AHERNE
   While representing Great Britain, broke the Olympic record by almost 2 feet (a feat comparable with the modern-day efforts of Bob Beamon in the 1968 long-jump), to win the 1908 Olympic Triple Jump with a leap of 48 feet 11¼ inches. His Olympic record lasted until 1924.

2. EDMOND BARRETT
   While representing the United Kingdom, was a member of the victorious Tug-of-War side for the City Police in the 1908 London Olympic Games. They beat the Liverpool Police side in the final.

3. JOSEPH DEAKIN
   Irish champion at both One Mile and Four Miles in 1901, won an Olympic Gold medal in 1908, when he was a member of the 3-Man 3-Mile Team race (ran over 4,828 metres). He actually won the race (in 14 minutes and 39.6 seconds), and his 2 fellow team members all finished in front of each member of the silver and bronze medal winners.

4. JOHN PIUS BOLAND
   Dublin-born tennis player representing Great Britain, won 2 gold medals (Men's Singles and Men's Doubles) at the inaugural games in Athens in 1896, thereby becoming the first Irish-born Olympic gold medal winner.

5. RONNIE DELANY

By winning the 1,500 metres title in Melbourne, Delany, a native of Arklow, became the most recent sportsman to win a gold medal in the Olympic Games while representing the Republic of Ireland. From a position of tenth at the bell, he came through the pack to beat the German Klaus Richthenhain in a time of 3:41:2, a new Olympic record.

6. JOHN FLANAGAN

Co Limerick-born United States policeman, won 3 Olympic Hammer titles in successive Olympiads, 1900, 1904 and 1908. He improved his winning throw on each occasion, starting at 167 feet 4 inches in Paris, and throwing 170 feet 41$\frac{1}{4}$ inches in London. He also won a gold medal with the United States Tug-of-War side of 1904.

7. JOHNNY HAYES

Irish-born, Bloomingdales clerk from New York, credited with winning the 1908 Olympic marathon in London, in a race more famous for the disqualification of the first-past-the-post, Dorando Pietri. Hayes's time of 2:55:18.4, although he finished more than half a minute behind the Italian, was still good enough to break the Olympic record.

8. BOBBY KERR

Enniskillen-born, Ontario fireman, won the 1908 Olympic 200 metres title under the Canadian flag, in a time of 22.6 seconds.

9. JIMMY KIRKWOOD

Lisnagarvey player, member of the Great Britain Hockey team which won a highly creditable gold medal at the Seoul Olympics of 1988.

10. CORNELIUS (CON) LEAHY

While representing Great Britain, won the (intercalary) 1906 running high jump title in Athens, clearing a height of 5 feet 91$\frac{7}{8}$ inches, and again in the 1908 games in London, clearing a much more respectable 6 feet 2 inches, claimed the bronze medal.

11. KENNETH McARTHUR
Ballymoney-born immigrant to South Africa in 1905; won the 1912 Stockholm title at the marathon, with what was then a respectable time of 2 hours, 36 minutes and 54.8 seconds.

12. PATRICK J. 'BABE' McDONALD
Irish-born United States athlete; won the 56lb weight throw at the Antwerp Games in August 1920, when he was 42 years old. This makes him the oldest athlete in the entire history of the Olympic Games to win a gold medal.

13. MATTHEW (MATT) McGRATH
Irish-born policeman; so dominant in winning the Stockholm Hammer title of 1912, that the shortest of his 6 throws was 15 feet longer than anyone else's in the competition's longest heave. Needless to say, he set an Olympic record in doing so, with his 179 feet 71/8 inches which lasted for 20 years.

14. STEPHEN MARTIN
Won a bronze medal with Great Britain in the 1984 Olympic Games in Los Angeles; went on to join Jimmy Kirkwood on the gold medal winning Hockey XI in Seoul in 1988.

15. PAT O'CALLAGHAN
Born Derrygallon, north Cork; won 2 Olympic gold medals in the Hammer event, at Amsterdam in 1928 (winning by 4 inches with a throw of 168 feet and 7 inches), and in Los Angeles in 1932 (winning by nearly 6 feet with a last throw of 176 feet 11 inches), becoming the only sportsman representing Ireland to win 2 Olympic titles.

16. PETER G. O'CONNOR
While representing Great Britain won the Triple Jump championship at the (intercalary) Athens games of 1906, with a jump of 46 feet 2½ inches. So proud of his native county was he that he climbed the flagpole and replaced the Union Jack flag by the Irish tricolour.

17. GEORGE CON O'KELLY
    Corkman; while representing the United Kingdom won the 1908 Olympic title at Heavyweight Wrestling, defeating a Norwegian, Jacob Gundersen in the final, having defeated in the third round fellow Corkman Edmond Barrett.

18. MARY PETERS
    Belfast-born; became the first Northern Ireland athlete to win an Olympic gold medal for her county when, in 1972 at Munich she broke the world record with 4,801 points for the Pentathlon and defeated the German local favourite, Heidi Rosendahl.

19. NOEL MARY PURCELL
    The only Irishman in a joint British-Irish side which won a controversial victory over the host nation Belgium by 3-2 in the final of the 1920 Olympic Water-Polo competition at Antwerp.

20. PADDY RYAN
    Born in Pallasgreen, Co Limerick; won the Olympic 16lb Hammer throw at the Antwerp Games of 1920 (while representing the United States), with a throw of 173 feet 5⅝ inches. This meant that the title had been won on each occasion since its inception in 1900 by an Irishman. If Pat O'Callaghan's 2 titles in 1928 and 1932 are included, it means that 7 of the first 8 Olympic Hammer titles were won by men born in Ireland.

21. MARTIN SHERIDAN
    Born in Co Mayo; won four Olympic gold medals while representing the United States. He won the Discus titles in 1904, (intercalary) 1906 and 1908, and won the Men's Shot Putt in 1906. In 1908 he also won the now-discontinued Greek-style Discus, with a throw of 124 feet and 8 inches.

22. BOB TISDALL
    Won the 1932 Olympic 400 metres Hurdles event at the Los Angeles Olympic Games, when, in only his seventh ever race over the distance, he beat the world record set by Glenn Hardin of the United States in the final, in a time of 51.7 seconds.

The Ring
Irish-born boxing World Champions

1. IKE O'NEILL WEIR (nicknamed the 'Belfast Spider')
   Featherweight, born in Lurgan, 1867; won the world title in 1890, making him the first world champion at his weight.

2. JACK 'NONPAREIL' DEMPSEY
   Born in Kildare 1862 (no relation to the great Heavyweight champion); the world's first Middleweight champion, taking the title in 1884. He held it until 1891, when Bob Fitzsimmons became the title holder.

3. JIMMY McLARNIN
   The only Irish-born boxer to hold a world title on 2 different occasions, doing so at Welterweight, in the 1930s. He won it first on 29 May 1933, by KO-ing Young Corbett III. Having lost the title a year later on points to Barney Ross, he regained it on 17 September 1934, by defeating Ross.

4. JACK McAULIFFE
   Born in Meelin, Co Cork; one of only 3 world title-holding boxers ever, never to have lost a fight (the other 2 are Rocky Marciano and the American James Barry). This Cork-born lightweight won his title in 1885, and held onto it for 11 years.

5. MIKE McTAIGUE
   The Ennis-born Clareman became, in 1923, the Light Heavyweight champion of the world when, after a 21-year career, he beat 'Battlin' Siki in Dublin. He held the title until 1925, when the championship was won by Paul Berlenbach.

6. GEORGE GARDNER
   Born in Lisdoonvarna, Co Clare 1872; Light Heavyweight boxer; won his world title in 1903, at the age of 31, to be succeeded by Bob Fitzsimmons.

7. JIMMY GARDNER

Lisdoonvarna-born Welterweight; claimed the world title in 1908. He won 51 bouts out of 100 bouts in a professional career stretching from 1900 to 1913.

8. TOM McCORMICK

Dundalk-born Welterweight; claimed the world title in 1914. During a short career of only 4 years, 1911–1915, he won 35 of his 46 contests.

9. DAVE SULLIVAN

Born in Cork 1877; won the Featherweight championship of the world on 28 September 1898, when his American opponent retired during their fight on Coney Island. Sullivan lost his title 46 days later, making him the shortest reigning Featherweight world champ in history.

10. RINTY MONAGHAN

Born in Belfast 1920; held the world Flyweight title for two years, 1948–1950, having beaten Jackie Patterson to take the title. When he won the European title in April 1949, he became the only boxer in history to hold 5 titles at the same weight simultaneously, as he was then also World, British, British Empire, and Irish champion Featherweight.

11. JOHNNY CALDWELL

Born in Befast 1938; won a disputed world title at Bantam weight in 1961, when he beat Alphonse Halimi of France. The title was only recognised in New York state and Europe. He lost the title in 1962.

12. BARRY McGUIGAN, the 'Clones Cyclone'

Won the world Featherweight title in 1984 when he defeated Eusebio Pedroza; lost it again in 1985 to Steve Cruz.

13. DAVE 'BOY' McAULEY

This Larne-born part-time chef made two gallant but unsuccessful attempts at the WBA World Flyweight Championship in 1986 and 1987, both against the Columbian, Fiel Castro. His luck finally changed in June 1989, when he outpointed the champion, Duke McKenzie, in the Wembley Arena, to obtain the IBF version of the world crown, thus making him the second Antrim man (besides Rinty Monaghan) to win a world boxing title.

GAA Champions
All-Ireland winners and losers

Below are listed, in order of most wins, the counties which have won All-Ireland Senior Football and Hurling titles. Alongside the winners is a list of counties which have not won the title.

Football

The 15 counties that have won All-Ireland SFC titles, and the 17 counties that have failed to do so

	Winners		Losers
1.	Kerry	30 titles	Antrim
2.	Dublin	21	Armagh
3.	Galway	7	Carlow
4.	Meath	6	Clare
5.	Wexford	5	Derry
6.	Cavan	5	Donegal
7.	Cork	5	Fermanagh
8.	Tipperary	4	Kilkenny
9.	Kildare	4	Leitrim
10.	Louth	3	Laois
11.	Mayo	3	Longford
12.	Down	3	Monaghan
13.	Offaly	3	Sligo
14.	Limerick	2	Tyrone
15.	Roscommon	2	Waterford
16.			Westmeath
17.			Wicklow

Hurling

The 12 counties (and London) that have won All-Ireland SHC titles, and the 20 that have (up to 1989) failed to do so

	Winners		Losers
1.	Cork	26 titles	Armagh
2.	Kilkenny	23	Antrim
3.	Tipperary	21	Carlow
4.	Limerick	7	Cavan
5.	Dublin	6	Derry
6.	Wexford	5	Donegal
7.	Galway	4	Down
8.	Waterford	2	Fermanagh
9.	Offaly	2	Kildare
10.	Clare	1	Leitrim
11.	Kerry	1	Longford
12.	Laois	1	Louth
13.	London	1	Mayo
14.			Meath
15.			Monaghan
16.			Roscommon
17.			Sligo
18.			Tyrone
19.			Westmeath
20.			Wicklow

Note that there are 11 counties that have won neither the football nor hurling crown. They are: Antrim, Armagh, Carlow, Derry, Donegal, Fermanagh, Leitrim, Longford, Monaghan, Sligo, Westmeath and Wicklow.

National Honours
18 Irish record-breaking sports cap winners

1. GERALDINE BARNIVILLE
   Born 7 November 1942; the Irish squash rackets player holds the women's world record number of international caps, when between 1973 and 1983 she represented Ireland on 71 occasions.

2. MARIE BARTLETT
   Irish ladies' hockey player; with 55 caps, the most capped player for her country.

3. LIAM BRADY
   Dublin-born Irish soccer mid-fielder; became the Republic of Ireland's most capped soccer international in 1987 when he surpassed the record 60 caps gained by Johnny Giles. His total number of appearances for his country will not be known until he retires.

4. OSSIE CALHOUN
   Irish cricket wicket-keeper; was capped 87 times for Ireland between the years 1959 and 1979, during which time he was never dropped by his country. He was Ireland's most capped cricketer from the mid-Seventies until August 1988, when surpassed by Michael Halliday.

5. J.B. (JOSEPH BOYNTON, or JOE) CARR
   Ireland's outstanding amateur golfer; won a record 10 Walker Cup appearances against the United States in 1947, 1949, 1951, 1953, 1955, 1957, 1959, 1963, 1965, and as non-playing captain in 1967. His 138 home international matches played for Ireland between 1947 and 1949 (only 50 of which he lost), makes him Irish amateurs' most capped player in this series.

6. MIKE GIBSON
   All-round Ireland rugby out-half and centre; with 69 caps between 1964 and 1979, the world's most capped rugby player. With the addition of his 12 Lions Test caps, his

total of 81 international caps against International board countries, is a record unlikely to be repeated for some time.

7. DAVID GOTTO
Born 1949; with 121 international appearances for Ireland, holds the world record for the most caps in the game of squash.

8. TERRY GREGG
Born 1950; Irish hockey player; played 102 times for Ireland, and 42 times for Great Britain, making him the most capped home international hockey player, until overtaken in 1988 by Richard Leman of England.

9. MICHAEL HALLIDAY
The Phoenix off-spin bowler; in August 1988, became at 39, Ireland's most capped cricketer, with 88 caps in 18 seasons from 1970 onwards. No mean batsman either, the teacher at Wesley College has taken over 184 wickets for Ireland, among them Mike Gatting, Geoff Boycott, Mike Brearly and Conrad Hunte.

10. PAT JENNINGS
Gentle giant Northern Ireland soccer goalkeeper; played for Watford, Tottenham Hotspur and Arsenal; capped 119 times for Northern Ireland between 1964 and 1986, giving him the world record for full internationals against other national teams. His 119th and last cap was against Brazil in the 1986 Mexico World Cup, on his 41st birthday, 12 June 1986.

11. DAVID JUDGE
Born 1936; hockey player, played for Ireland 124 times between 1957 and 1978. He also represented Great Britain 15 times, which made him, at 139 caps, the game's most capped home countries player, until surpassed by Terry Gregg in the number of combined caps.

12. TOM KIERNAN
Ireland, Munster and Cork Constitution full-back, was the world's most capped rugby player, with 54 caps, for a period in the early 1970s.

13. JACKIE KYLE
    Ireland outside half of the glory years of Irish rugby of the late 1940s and early 1950s; won 46 caps for his country between 1947 and 1958. From that latter year, for a period of 13 years, he was the world's most capped rugby player.

14. WILLIE JOHN McBRIDE
    Ireland, Ulster and Ballymena rugby second row forward; represented the British and Irish Lions in more test matches than any other player in history. Between 1962 and 1974, he played 17 test matches, his nearest rival being English scrum-half, Dickie Jeeps, with 13 appearances. Also for a period between 1974 and 1979, he was the world's most capped player, with 63 caps.

15. MARY McKENNA
    Irish amateur golfer; has won a record 9 Curtis Cup caps, representing the British and Irish Ladies' golfers in the bi-annual match against the United States. Her appearances were consecutive in 1970, 1972, 1974, 1976, 1978, 1980, 1982, 1984 and 1986.

16. CHRISTY O'CONNOR
    The 'Maestro'; won an amazing, probably never to be equalled, 10 consecutive Ryder Cup places, during his career in the world of professional golf. The years of his appearances were 1955, 1957, 1959, 1961, 1963, 1965, 1967, 1969, 1971 and 1973.

17. SAM THOMPSON
    Irish Bowls player; has the greatest number of outdoor international appearances by any bowler, achieved in the period between 1947 and 1973. At the age of 61 he achieved the world record of 78 outdoor international caps. His record was equalled by England's David Bryant in 1987. Thompson also won 50 indoor caps.

18. JUNE WIGHTMAN
    Holds the world record for international appearances in Netball, having, between 1964 and 1985, represented Northern Ireland on 90 occasions.

SIGNING OFF

Pen Names
Irish pseudonyms, noms-de-plume and nicknames

Real name	Also known as
Molly Allgood	Maire O'Neill
Arnold Bax	Dermot O'Byrne
Dionysius Lardner Boursiquot	Dion Boucicault Lee Moreton Bourcicault
John Brennan	Mrs Sidney Czira
Rosemary Brown	Dana
Edmund Burke	The Dinner Bell
Daniel Patrick Carroll	Danny La Rue
John Casey	Sean O'Casey The Green Crow
Ada Crehan	Ada Rehan
Barbara Dickson	Dick (from Maxi, Dick & Twink)
David Evans	The Edge
Cicely Isobel Fairfield	Rebecca West
John Fitzgibbon, Earl of Clare	Black Jack Fitzgibbon
Maureen FitzSimmons	Maureen O'Hara The Queen of Technicolour Baby Elephant
Marie Dolores Eliza Rosanna Gilbert	Lola Montez Countess of Landsfeldt
Oliver St John Gogarty	The Green Fool

Reverend James Owen Hannay	George A. Birmingham
Paul Hewson	Bono
Reginald Ingram Montgomery Hitchcock	Rex Ingram
Douglas Hyde	'An Craoibhin Aoibhinn'
Edward Noel Kelly	Nicky Kelly
James Plunkett Kelly	James Plunkett
Adele King	Twink
Jack Keyes Byrne	Hugh Leonard
Cecil Day Lewis	Nicholas Blake
Irene McCaubrey	Maxi
J. P. McManus	The Sundance Kid
Luke McMasters	Giant Haystacks
William Maginn	Ensign O'Doherty
Reverend Francis Sylvester Mahony	Father Prout
Richard Martin	Humanity Dick
Violet Francis Martin	Martin Ross
Conor Cruise O'Brien	Donat O'Donnell
Daniel O'Connell	'The Liberator'
Timothy Power O'Connor	Tay Pay O'Connor
Michael O'Donovan	Frank O'Connor
Brian O'Nolan	Flann O'Brien Myles na Gopaleen
Raymond O'Sullivan	Gilbert O'Sullivan
Charles Stewart Parnell	The Chief
George Bernard Shaw	Corno Di Basseto
Brendan Francis Liam Pius Shiels	Brush Shiels
William Shields	Barry Fitzgerald

Sean Sherrard	Johnny Logan
Michael Sinnott	Mack Sennet
Abraham Stoker	Bram Stoker
Jonathan Swift	Isaac Bickerstaff; M'Flor O'Squarr; S.P.A.M.; M.B. Drapier; A Person of Honour; Student of Astronomy; Jack Frenchman; T.N. Philomath; Tinker; T. Fribble; Presto; Dr Andrew Tripe; Lemuel Gulliver; Abel Ripper; Simon Wagstaff; Gregory Miso-Sarum; A. Shoeboy; 'The Great Dean'
John Whelan	Sean O'Faolain
Lady Jane Francesca Wilde (née Elgin)	Speranza
Oscar Fingal Wills O'Flahertie Wilde	C.3.3. Sebastian Melmouth
Michael Willmore	Micheal Mac Liammoir

Signature Tunes

9 famous songs of other countries written by Irishmen

1. ALL THINGS BRIGHT AND BEAUTIFUL
   Celebrated Church of England hymn; composed by the Wicklow-born Cecilia Frances Alexander, whose other works include 'There is a Green Hill Far Away'.

2. DARBY AND JOAN
   Very British sentimental song; written by Offaly-born James Lynam Molloy (1837–1909). It was very widely in vogue. Other songs he composed were 'The Kerry Dances', 'Love's Old Sweet Song', and 'Just a Song at Twilight'.

3. GOD SAVE NEW ZEALAND
   New Zealand national anthem; written in 1878 by the immigrant Irish poet, Thomas Bracken.

4. RED SAILS IN THE SUNSET
   Enormously popular world-wide; written by Jimmy Kennedy (born in Omagh, Co Tyrone); inspired by the view of Portstewart Bay in evening time.

5. IRELAND BOYS HURRAY
   Written by Bantry-born T.D. O'Sullivan (1827–1914), the song has a strange place in American history. On the eve of the Battle of Fredericksburg in the Civil War of 1862, some soldiers from the Northern camp began to sing the song. Their opponents from the South took up the chorus, and for a strange half an hour, both armies sang the words 'Here's to Ireland, Dear old Ireland, Ireland Boys Hurray'. O'Sullivan also wrote the patriotic 'God Save Ireland'.

6. THE RED FLAG
   The anthem for socialists, Labour parties and Trade Unions; originally composed and written to an Irish tune, 'The White Cockade', by the Kilskrye, Co Meath-born, Jim Connell. Many years later however the British Labour Party, while retaining Connell's lyrics, changed the tune to that of 'Tannenbaum'.

7. THE STAR SPANGLED BANNER
   National anthem of the United States; written by Francis Scott Key while witnessing the bombardment of Fort McHenry, at Baltimore, Maryland in September 1814. But it is claimed that the air for the song, which is supposed to be 'Anacreon in Heaven', was in fact an eighteenth-century marching air of the Royal Inniskilling Fusiliers of Enniskillen. This point is much debated.

8. THREE CHEERS FOR THE RED, WHITE AND BLUE
   Patriotic British song; in fact composed by the Clare-born convicted Fenian and Young Irelander, Stephen Meaney (1825–1888).

9. WHEN JOHNNY COMES MARCHING HOME
   Associated with both the American Civil War and the Spanish-American Wars; written, words and music, by the Irish-born bandmaster, Patrick S. (Sarsfield) Gilmore.

Shipwrecked

21 noted Irish people who came to a watery grave

1. THOMAS ANDREWS

   Noted Irish shipbuilder; aboard the *Titanic* in 1912, a ship which he designed and helped to build; on its maiden voyage the ship hit an iceberg and sank; Andrews was one of the 1,503 people to perish.

2. O'BRIEN BUTLER

   Composer of the first opera in Irish, 'Muirgheis'; one of 1,198 to lose their lives on board the *Lusitania,* when the Cunard Line steamer was torpedoed and sunk by a German submarine off Kinsale in 1915.

3. BRIAN DONN BYRNE

   New York-born Irish novelist; drowned in Courtmacsharry Bay, Co Cork, on 19 June 1928, when the car he was travelling in ran off the road. He was buried at Rathclarion, Coolmain.

4. JAMES CAREY

   Informer on the Invincibles, involved in the Phoenix Park Murders of Cavendish and Burke; was on a voyage on the *Melrose Castle* between Capetown and Natal in 1883, when a bricklayer, Patrick O'Donnell, assassinated him by shooting him when the ship was off Capetown. O'Donnell, an Invincible, was hanged in London.

5. WILLIAM CRAIG

   Irish landscape painter in water colours; accidentally drowned in Lake George, the picturesque United States resort in the Adirondack Mountains of New York State on 26 August 1875.

6. JAMES G. FARRELL

   Novelist; author of 'Troubles', stricken with polio; was fishing off Bantry Bay in August 1979, during the Fastnet race week, when a freak wave knocked him into the water. As he was not strong enough to save himself, he drowned.

7. MICHAEL ANGELO HAYES
Irish painter; on 31 December 1877 he drowned at the age of 57, when he fell into a water tank that he was inspecting on top of his house.

8. RICHARD HEAD
Carrickfergus-born writer; most famous work was the loosely autobiographical 'The English Rogue'; drowned in the Solent off the south coast of England, at the age of 49.

9. SIR HUGH LANE
Art collector and critic; returning from the United States on board the *Lusitania*, when it sank off Kinsale on 7 May 1915.

10. BASIL MATURIN
Dublin-born preacher and writer; also on board the *Lusitania* when it sank. He was returning from a preaching tour of the United States for Lent of that year.

11. THOMAS MEAGHER
Young Irelander; serving as Secretary of Montana Territory in the United States; while returning to explore the Northern Territory for the second time he fell off his ship in strange circumstances and drowned in the Mississippi river on 1 July 1867.

12. ERNEST MOERAN
Irish composer; drowned in the Kenmare River, his body being found there on 1 December 1950.

13. EDWARD NEWELL
Informer; was just about to get on board a ship to America with the wife of a friend, when he was assassinated in 1798. He was not quite 27 years old.

14. MUIRIS O'SUILLEABHAIN
Author of 'Fiche Bliain Ag Fas' (Twenty Years-A Growing); drowned while bathing in Galway Bay, off Connemara, on 25 January 1950. He was 46.

15. ANNA PARNELL
Land agitator, and younger sister of Charles Stewart; was living in retirement in England, when on 11 September 1911, at the age of 59, she went swimming, against the advice of friends, in a rough sea at Ilfracombe and drowned.

16. THE 1st VISCOUNT PIRRIE
Quebec-born Belfast shipbuilder; controlled the largest ship-building firm in the world, Harland and Wolff, and was responsible for building the *Titanic,* the *Teutonic* and the *Oceanic;* died at sea, at the age of 77, on 7 June 1924.

17. WILLIAM TYRONE POWER
Actor, and great-grandfather of the matinée idol Tyrone Power; was 44 when he got on board the largest steamer afloat, *The President,* on 11 March 1841. However, on St Patrick's Day, a huge gale resulted in the ship floundering, and all on board were lost.

18. SEAN RUSSELL
Chief of Staff of the Irish Republican Army 1938–1939; was travelling to Ireland on board a German U-Boat, when on 8 August 1940, he died aged 47. He was buried at sea about 100 miles out of Galway Bay. Frank Ryan, his adversary, a socialist republican, who accompanied him on the journey, was returned to Germany.

19. PATRICK J. SAUL
Pioneer Irish aviator; died while fishing on Lough Swilly, on the 27 June 1968. His wife had died in 1922 when a ship he had commanded sank off France.

20. THOMAS STEELE
'Head Pacificator' for Daniel O'Connell; landlord, and supporter of Repeal; on hearing of O'Connell's death, tried to commit suicide by jumping off Waterloo Bridge in London. He was rescued from the river, but the injuries he received resulted in his death a few days later.

21. ELLIOT WARBURTON
Tullamore-born novelist; perished off Land's End in a fire on board the mail steamer *Amazon,* which was on its maiden voyage to the West Indies, on 4 January 1852. By extraordinary coincidence, Warburton had a historical novel, 'Darien, or the Merchant Prince', published later in the same year, which describes the horrors of a fire at sea.

Poignant, Pithy, Pathetic, Proud – and Irish

Last words attributed to famous Irish people

BRENDAN BEHAN
Speaking to a nun, he said, 'Thank you sister, may you be the mother of a bishop.'

ROGER CASEMENT
In his last letter he wrote, 'It is a cruel thing to die with all men understanding.'

VISCOUNT CASTLEREAGH, ROBERT STEWART
'Bankhead, I have opened my neck. Let me fall upon your arm. It's all over.'

ERSKINE CHILDERS
Author of 'Riddle of the Sands'; facing the firing squad, he said to them, 'Take a step or two forward, lads; it will be easier that way.'

MICHAEL COLLINS
a) 'Come on boys, there they are, running up the road.'
b) 'Forgive them.'

JAMES CONNOLLY
'I say a prayer for all men who do their duty according to their lights.'

EDWARD 'NED' DALY
About to be executed for his part in the Easter Rising of 1916; said, 'Tell Uncle John I did my best.'

THOMAS DERMODY (1775–1803)
'I am vicious because I like it.'

ROBERT EMMET
Three times he was asked by his executioner if he was ready, and each time he replied, 'Not yet.'

SEAMUS FORDE
Painter; dying at the age of 23, his last written words were 'I am very weak.'

ROBERT ROLLO GILLESPIE
When shot through the heart, he said, 'One shot more for the honour of Down.'

OLIVER ST JOHN GOGARTY
'I think my trouble is coming to me.'

OLIVER GOLDSMITH
When asked by a Dr Truton whether his mind was at ease, he replied, 'No, it is not!'

MAUD GONNE
'I feel now an ineffable joy.'

HENRY GRATTAN
'I die with a love of liberty in my heart, and this declaration in favour of my country in my hand.'

REX INGRAM
Irish-born Hollywood film director; when his wife, Alice Terry, visited him on her birthday, he said, 'I will see you in the morning. Be sure and pick out something pretty.'

JAMES JOYCE
'Does anybody understand?'

EOIN MacNEILL
When he heard somebody at his bedside say, 'He will not need prayers', he retorted, 'Everybody needs prayers.'

SIR ROBERT MONTEITH
The 'Mystery Man of Banna Strand'; in a conversation with his wife Molly; 'Is that you Molly?' 'Yes.' 'Where are you.' 'I'm right here by your pillow.' 'You would be.'

HENRY MUNROE
United Irishman; 'Tell my country I deserved better from it.'

TURLOUGH O'CAROLAN
Ireland's legendary harpist; when asking for a last glass of whiskey on his deathbed, and not being able to drink it, he kissed the cup and said, 'It would be hard if such friends should pass at least without kissing.'

FRANK O'CONNOR
'I hope you don't expect me to entertain you.'

JIMMY O'DEA
His last words on stage were, 'Farewell, my friends, I'll see you all one day in Glocamara.'

CHARLES STEWART PARNELL
a) To his wife, Kitty O'Shea, he said, 'Kiss me, sweet Wifey, and I will sleep a little.'
b) 'Let my love be given to my colleagues, and to the people of Ireland.'

EDEL QUINN 'Jesus! Jesus!'

GEORGE BERNARD SHAW
a) To his nurse, Gwendoline Howell, he said, 'Sister, you are trying to keep me alive as an old curiosity. But I'm done. I'm finished. I'm going to die.'
b) To Ellen Casey, 'Well, it will be a new experience, anyway.'
c) When Mrs Laden said to him that she wished it was she that was dying and not him, he replied, 'You wouldn't if you knew what I've had to put up with.'

RICHARD BRINSLEY SHERIDAN
'I am absolutely undone and broken hearted.'

LAWRENCE STERNE
Clonmel-born novelist; 'Now it is done.'

JONATHAN SWIFT
'I am dying like a poisoned rat in a hole. I am what I am. I am what I am.'

JOHN MILLINGTON SYNGE
'It is no use fighting death any longer.'

THE DUKE OF WELLINGTON
When asked if he would like some tea, he replied, 'Yes if you please.'

THEOBALD WOLFE TONE
When his doctor told him that the slightest movement would kill him, he said, 'I can yet find words to thank you, sir; it is the most welcome news you could give me. What should I wish to live for?'

OSCAR WILDE
a) 'That wallpaper is killing me. One of us must go.'
b) 'I am dying as I have lived, beyond my means.'